About This Book

Why is this topic important?

Training is at a crossroads. In a recent High Performance Workforce Study conducted by Accenture (2004), 40 percent of chief executive officers and chief financial officers were either ambivalent about or dissatisfied with their training organizations, and only 16 percent were highly satisfied with training's ability to ensure that their learning output was meeting business requirements. The perceptions of these corporate executives who approve budgets and set corporate strategy have grave implications for training organizations. Six Sigma has both the respect of business executives and a proven record for developing products that meet both business and customer requirements. This book provides training professionals with the tools required to integrate Six Sigma methodology into their current training development process.

What can you achieve with this book?

This book provides training professionals with a clear understanding of the shortcomings of current popular training development models. It then introduces them to the world of Six Sigma and the tool set that previously was available only to quality or process improvement professionals. Finally, it introduces training professionals to a new development methodology that combines the best of both Six Sigma and instructional system design (ISD). Using the tools and techniques contained in this book will position readers to gain the respect of business stakeholders and develop training programs where the learning output meets business requirements.

How is this book organized?

This book has three parts. Part One introduces ISD and Six Sigma, points out the strengths and weaknesses of the two approaches, and examines the rationale for combining the methodologies. Part Two introduces training professionals to DMADDI, a new Six Sigma model tailored to the development of training programs, and a tool set that they can immediately put into practice. Part Three presents a case study documenting the experience that one company had in applying Six Sigma methodology to its e-learning process. Although the approach used by this organization was the improvement approach (DMAIC) as opposed to the design methodology approach (DMADDI), many of the tools and techniques used in this project are applicable to both processes. The case study will give the reader a good idea of what they can expect the first time they apply a Six Sigma approach to a training project.

About Pfeiffer

Pfeiffer serves the professional development and hands-on resource needs of training and human resource practitioners and gives them products to do their jobs better. We deliver proven ideas and solutions from experts in HR development and HR management, and we offer effective and customizable tools to improve workplace performance. From novice to seasoned professional, Pfeiffer is the source you can trust to make yourself and your organization more successful.

Essential Knowledge   Pfeiffer produces insightful, practical, and comprehensive materials on topics that matter the most to training and HR professionals. Our Essential Knowledge resources translate the expertise of seasoned professionals into practical, how-to guidance on critical workplace issues and problems. These resources are supported by case studies, worksheets, and job aids and are frequently supplemented with CD-ROMs, Web sites, and other means of making the content easier to read, understand, and use.

Essential Tools   Pfeiffer's Essential Tools resources save time and expense by offering proven, ready-to-use materials—including exercises, activities, games, instruments, and assessments—for use during a training or team-learning event. These resources are frequently offered in looseleaf or CD-ROM format to facilitate copying and customization of the material.

Pfeiffer also recognizes the remarkable power of new technologies in expanding the reach and effectiveness of training. While e-hype has often created whizbang solutions in search of a problem, we are dedicated to bringing convenience and enhancements to proven training solutions. All our e-tools comply with rigorous functionality standards. The most appropriate technology wrapped around essential content yields the perfect solution for today's on-the-go trainers and human resource professionals.

www.pfeiffer.com

Essential resources for training and HR professionals

DEVELOPING AND MEASURING TRAINING THE SIX SIGMA WAY

A Business Approach to Training and Development

Kaliym A. Islam

Foreword by Edward A. Trolley

A Wiley Imprint
www.pfeiffer.com

Published by Pfeiffer
An Imprint of Wiley
989 Market Street, San Francisco, CA 94103-1741
www.pfeiffer.com

For additional copies/bulk purchases of this book in the U.S. please contact 800-274-4434.

Pfeiffer books and products are available through most bookstores. To contact Pfeiffer directly call our Customer Care Department within the U.S. at 800-274-4434, outside the U.S. at 317-572-3985, fax 317-572-4002, or visit www.pfeiffer.com.

Pfeiffer also publishes its books in a variety of electronic formats. Some content that appears in print may not be available in electronic books.

Chapter Twelve is published by permission of *LTI Magazine* and was originally published on March 23, 2003.

Library of Congress Cataloging-in-Publication Data

Islam, Kaliym A.
Developing and measuring training the six sigma way: a business approach to training and development/Kaliym A. Islam; foreword by Edward A. Trolley
     p. cm.
  Includes bibliographical references and index.
  ISBN-13: 978-0-7879-8533-2 (alk. paper)
  ISBN-10: 0-7879-8533-3 (alk. paper)
  1. Employees—Training of. 2. Six sigma (Quality control standard) I. Title.
  HF5549.5.T7I78 2006
  658.3'12404—dc22

                                                  2006016673

Acquiring Editor: Matthew Davis
Director of Development: Kathleen Dolan Davies
Developmental Editor: Susan Rachmeler
Production Editor: Rachel Anderson
Editor: Beverly Miller

Manufacturing Supervisor: Becky Carreño
Editorial Assistant: Samya Sattar
Cover Design: Jeff Puda
Illustrations: Lotus Art

Printed in the United States of America
Printing   10 9 8 7 6 5 4 3 2 1

CONTENTS

FIGURES, TABLES, AND EXHIBITS

FOREWORD

Edward A. Trolley

If training professionals are to consistently develop training programs that solve business problems, deliver a quantifiable return on investment, and justify the existence of the training department, they must adopt a business methodology as a model for development.

KALIYM A. ISLAM

EXACTLY, Kaliym! This book and its author, Kaliym Islam, build the business case for the necessity of following a proven, reliable, and consistent business methodology for ensuring that training is relevant, is driven by the needs of the business, and delivers quantifiable value. This is a how-to book for training professionals who have struggled for years to become full business partners with their customers and deliver the same levels of value that their customers realize from other investments they make.

It seems as if every week I see another article or another book on the subject of measuring the value of training. And it seems as if they all share the same belief that the measurement process kicks in after the training is over. And it seems as if every year, the American Society for Training and Development (ASTD) annual report shows little to no change in what organizations are measuring and the methodologies they are using to measure.

I have yet to find a CEO of a large company who knows how much he or she is spending on training and, worse, what value he or she is receiving from what is likely a large investment. The cost part is easy to understand. Training in most organizations is highly dispersed, everybody does it, the spending is rarely captured in one place, and in many situations, the spending doesn't even show up on a training line item in the budget. So I can rationalize why this situation exists even though I believe it should be resolved. What I cannot understand is how a business can continue to spend large amounts of money on training without a clear line of sight as to how that investment is going to help the business. The real truth is that the tide has turned, and businesspeople will not continue to throw money at something where the value is unclear. They have too many other places to put that money where they are confident of some sort of return.

See the connection? They don't know, and we sure aren't helping them! Maybe that's why training is one of the first expenses to be cut when things get tough.

This has been going on for so long that it tells me that the current measurement methodology is flawed. It's a fifty-year-old methodology that was created when training was a nice thing to do, and it is not being held to the same standards as any other large investments that companies make.

If we are ever going to move training from the backroom to the boardroom, then we have to start thinking like businesspeople—that is, like our customers. What I love about this book is that it is based on the premise that customers of training must define their expectations and how they will quantify the value they expect to receive from the investment they make in training. And it must be all of these customers, not just the employee who receives the training. Underlying the entire concept of *Running Training Like a Business* (a book I coauthored in 1999) is a commitment by training to measure what matters. And what matters are effectiveness and efficiency. In business, that's what always matters. And your customers will define it in terms like percentage of market share growth, increased revenue amount, percentage of productivity improvement, growth in customer satisfaction, or amount of cost reduction because those matter to them.

The book also establishes a premise that we must use a business-oriented methodology to identify stakeholder requirements for training and design and deliver training products that meet those requirements. Islam has developed the DMADDI model, which combines the best of Six Sigma, design for Six Sigma, and instructional systems design to ensure that training is driven by what is important to its customers, is clear about what needs to be learned, and is then designed in a way that delivers to employees what they need in a way that ensures that they learn something.

There likely isn't a businessperson around who hasn't been exposed to Six Sigma methodology. Islam has moved Six Sigma out of manufacturing, where everything has a sharp business edge, to training, where the edges are rounded. This Six Sigma–based model will be the "knife sharpener" for training. It will advance the proposition that training investments must deliver the same types of business results as any other business investment and will help organizations forever answer the question, "What value am I getting from my investment in training?"

My hope is that this book will be read by every training professional and leader who wants to make certain that the work he or she does makes a real and tangible business difference for customers, the organization, the business, or the company. To restate an old saying, "If you don't know where you are going, any road will take you there." Kaliym Islam is showing us how to ensure we understand the destination before we begin the journey. Every businessperson who engages with a training professional will value being asked, "What business objective or goal are you trying to accomplish, and what measures will you use to determine whether this is a good investment for you?" *before* being asked to commit funds. Why? Because that is what their customers ask of them.

To Cathy, my loving wife and soul mate, for sharing your time with me so that I could complete this effort. I love you.

PREFACE

A well-seasoned and much decorated battleship captain was on his final voyage. As his ship headed to port for the final time, a great fog covered that section of the ocean. Worse, the ship's automated navigation system wasn't working. Many of the ship's junior officers became worried. The captain, thinking that this would be an excellent opportunity to teach one final lesson of the trip to his junior officers, took control of the manual navigation system and began directing the ship. The junior officers looked on in awe. None of them had ever had to direct a battleship manually. The captain beamed with pride as he began to bring the ship home. The fog, however, continued to get worse. Visibility was down to about thirty feet. The captain wasn't worried at all. During his thirty years of duty, he had experienced virtually any situation that a battleship captain could endure. He was sure that he could handle a little fog.

Suddenly a panicked junior officer ran into the command center. "Captain" he said urgently. "There's something out there. There's a bright light directly in front of us. If we continue on this course, we'll crash right into whatever it is."

The captain remained calm. He smiled and asked the officer to pass him the ship's radio. "Son," he said, "don't sweat the small stuff." The captain turned the radio to the general frequency and then calmly announced, "This is Captain Johnson of the USS *Hybrid*. It seems as though we're on a collision course. I need you to adjust your course thirty degrees to the south."

There was silence on the line. Tension filled the command center. If something didn't happen soon, there would surely be a collision. Finally a response came back on the radio: "That's a negative, captain. You need to adjust your course thirty degrees south."

The captain was insulted. Never in his thirty years of naval service had anyone had the nerve to challenge his command. The junior officers looked on, wondering what the captain would do.

The captain again picked up the radio and this time in a more commanding voice said, "This is Captain Rufus Johnson of the U.S. battleship *Hybrid*. Son, I'm telling you that you need to change your course thirty degrees south now."

The junior officers stood silent waiting to hear what the response would be. And then it came: "No, *you* change your course thirty degrees south." The collective jaws of everyone in the command center dropped. Never had they heard anyone speak to their commanding officer in such a way.

The captain, now visibly upset, replied. "Son, I am Captain Rufus Johnson. I am the most decorated officer in the history of the navy. I am commanding a U.S. battleship with enough explosives to blow you into next week. For the last time, I am ordering you to adjust your course thirty degrees south."

Again there was silence on the line. The tension in the command center was so thick that you could cut it with a knife. Finally, after what seemed like an eternity, a response came across the radio: "Captain, this is a light house on an island that has been in this ocean for about a thousand years, and if you don't adjust your course, we're gonna have a collision."

The captain, with this new-found perspective, wisely adjusted the ship's course and avoided a catastrophe.

The story of the battleship is analogous to situations that training managers face in attempting to show the return on investment of training programs. During the interaction between training professionals and their business counterparts, the training professional (like the captain) comes to the table armed with years of experience at his or her craft, which tends to be instructional design or training or organizational development. He or she also tends to approach the interaction solely from that perspective. Unlike the captain who avoided the catastrophe, all too often the training professional fails to adjust course. The result all too frequently is a dissatisfied customer and a training program that is again forced to try and prove its value to the business or to justify its budget.

One option for training professionals who wish to avoid the experience of the battleship captain is to abandon or modify the traditional approach to developing training programs and embrace a more business-centric tactic. Six Sigma has proven successful at identifying the perspectives of all process stakeholders, identifying their requirements, and producing products that meet those requirements.

Because of its customer focus, Six Sigma provides ideal solutions for showing and proving the business impact of training. One immediate benefit of applying Six Sigma is the business credibility that the methodology brings. Because it is a non-training proprietary approach, Six Sigma is universally accepted by businesses across many industries. Had the captain of the battleship been a Six Sigma Black Belt, his junior officers would have never experienced the altercation that occurred in the story and could have focused on the main objective: bringing the ship to port.

July 2006

Kaliym A. Islam
Plainfield, New Jersey

ACKNOWLEDGMENTS

I acknowledge the following individuals for helping to make this book a reality: Ed Trolley, for starting the conversation on running training like a business; Tim Sosbe, Doug Harward, Haig Armaghanian, Barbara Sealund, Gail Pappas, Ara Ohanian, and Dale A. Hartwig for believing in a vision; Bill Aimetti, for seeing something in me and giving me an opportunity; Bill Scotto for being a great coach; Sam Kasmanoff for ongoing support; Michael Utvich, Seth Fleishman, and Nashid Salahuddin for valuable input and willingness to give ongoing feedback; Anne Palmer, for guiding me through this entire process, Matt Davis for being a champion and believing in this process, and Rosemary Kurtti and Kevin Carey for believing in radical change.

INTRODUCTION

Open the pages of any training publication, and you are guaranteed to find at least one article addressing how to prove return on investment. Attend any industry conference, and you will find several presentations that explore methodologies claiming to prove the business impact of training. The fact that there is still a need for so many articles and presentations indicates that the training profession has yet to establish a common methodology and tool set that successfully develops programs that are able to show the impact that training has on an organization (at least not in a manner that business professionals accept and respect).

The futility of previous development methodologies can be summed up by looking at some of the findings of a 2004 workforce survey conducted by Accenture where the business executives who participated indicated that measuring the effectiveness of learning was the number one challenge for the training organization. The same executives were less than satisfied with their training organization's ability to communicate the value of learning across the organization. The learning executives who took part in this survey indicated that they themselves must overcome a number of legacy restrictions, processes, metrics, and techniques that were fine for an approach to learning a decade or two ago, but are no longer adequate, and that the best practice human resource process revealed that companies must "first and foremost have a clear understanding of the importance of linking HR and training programs to business objectives. And in many cases, this linkage is based on the ability to accurately measure the impact of these programs on those objectives." (p. 35).

Six Sigma is a methodology that is universally accepted by businesses across various industries. Applying Six Sigma methodology to the development of training programs provides training professionals with a tremendous opportunity to develop programs in a way that overcomes the legacy restrictions, processes, metrics, and techniques that are no longer adequate and allows training professionals to communicate the value of learning across the organization.

If you are a training professional at any level in an organization who is frustrated because the training programs that you are delivering do not receive the recognition that they deserve, this book is for you. If you are frustrated because the business executives you are having conversations with seem to be speaking a different language, this book is for you. And if you are looking for a development methodology that provides techniques, metrics, and processes that resonate with the decision makers in your organization, this book is for you.

Developing and Measuring Training the Six Sigma Way identifies the shortcomings of today's most popular training development methodology, instructional system design (ISD), and explains why this approach is unable to identify and translate the business requirements for training programs in a way that business stakeholders respect. It examines the evaluation technique that is used by the majority of training professionals today and describes why this method has been unsuccessful at convincing business stakeholders that training programs are having a positive impact on the business. Finally, it presents a new design for Six Sigma technique—Define, Measure, Analyze, Design, Develop, Implement (DMADDI)—which successfully identifies business requirements, develops evaluation criteria that ensure there are predetermined quantifiable and objective standards agreed to by all project stakeholders, and provides a true measure of the effectiveness of the learning program, thus producing training programs that meet the needs of all program stakeholders.

This book is divided into three parts. Readers can start any place that makes sense for them.

The first three chapters, which comprise Part One, give a history and background of ISD and Six Sigma and explain the rationale for combining the two methodologies. Chapter One focuses on ISD. It explores the purpose and history of this approach to developing training programs and uncovers why the methodology has been unable to produce results that meet the expectations of business executives. Chapter Two introduces training professionals to the world of Six Sigma. It presents a history of the methodology and describes the different Six Sigma models. Chapter Three then makes the case for combining these two approaches.

Part Two introduces training professionals to a new Six Sigma model, DMADDI, which is tailored for the development of training programs. After an overview in Chapter Four, each of the next six chapters walks readers through a phase of the DMADDI model. As readers progress through Part Two, they will be made aware of both the similarities and the differences between the ISD and the Six Sigma approaches to designing training programs. Training professionals will be exposed to a new tool set they can immediately put into practice.

Part Three presents a case study documenting the experience that one company had in applying Six Sigma methodology to its e-learning process. Although the approach used by this organization was the improvement approach (DMAIC) as opposed to the design methodology approach (DFSS), many of the tools and techniques used in this project are applicable to both processes and many of the team concepts are similar. The case study will give the reader a good idea of what they can expect the first time they apply a Six Sigma approach to a training project.

PART ONE

THE BACKGROUND

CHAPTER ONE

WHY ISD HAS DIFFICULTY ADDRESSING BUSINESS ISSUES

Instructional systems design (ISD) is at the core of any training program. Virtually every training program that is developed today is done using ISD or some variation of it. As an approach to designing engaging instruction, ISD is unrivaled. As a methodology for developing training programs that address business issues, it doesn't work.

Contemporary thinking has sparked increased concern on the part of business professionals about the ability of programs developed using this methodology to address business issues or solve real business problems. This concern has affected the perception that corporate executives have of their training organizations. According to an Accenture 2004 workforce survey, 40 percent of the CEOs who participated were either ambivalent or dissatisfied with their company's training function. These same executives also rated boosting workforce productivity and agility as the most important training initiative, but only 17 percent of those were very satisfied with their training function's ability to deliver in that area. It has been said that perception is reality. The perception of the executives from the Accenture survey gives training professionals a disturbing reality: training programs developed using the ISD methodology are not producing results that are meeting the expectations of business executives.

In fact, ISD was never intended to address business issues; the process itself is devoid of techniques that are dedicated to addressing business concerns. Although there are several variations of ISD, each suffers from the same flaw: a lack of tools and techniques dedicated to solving business problems.

This chapter explores why ISD doesn't do a good job of addressing business issues or solving real business problems. It begins with an overview of the ISD methodology that will make clear what ISD was actually intended to accomplish. It then briefly explores the history of this approach to developing training programs, which will uncover why the methodology has been less than successful. Finally, it looks at two popular variations of this approach that claim to produce effective training programs and exposes the weaknesses of those approaches.

What Is ISD?

Instructional systems design is a methodology or process that educators and training professionals use to design instruction. According to Kevin Kruse, the e-learning guru, it is "the most widely used methodology for developing new training programs" (http://www.e-learningguru.com/articles/art2_1.htm). The stated purpose of ISD is to improve human performance, and the methodology is based on the premise that learning should not occur in a disorganized way; rather, it should be developed in harmony with methodical processes, tailored to a target audience, and have measurable outcomes. The popular glossary of terms, also powered by e-learningguru.com, describes ISD as the "[t]erm describing the systematic use of principles of instruction to ensure that learners acquire the skills and knowledge essential for successful completion of overtly specified performance goals" (http://www.e-learningguru.com/glossary/i.htm). Similar descriptions or understandings of ISD can be found in the corporate sector and academia. ICF Consulting asserts that "ISD consists of analyzing what is to be learned, planning an intervention that establishes the conditions for learning, and producing and refining instructional or non-instructional interventions until the specified performance objectives are met" (http://www.icfconsulting.com/Services/Training/trng-isd.asp). And the Southern Illinois University education program states that "Instructional Systems design basically focuses on how systems engineering can be applied toward the design of effective instruction" (http://www.siue.edu/~dknowlt/IT510/IT510_main.html). According to these and other definitions, the purpose of ISD is to ensure effective instruction, not to solve business problems or result in business impact. Because of its intended purpose, the methodology is equipped with tools, techniques, and approaches dedicated to ensuring effective instruction but lacking the components needed for achieving business goals.

History of ISD

As a formal discipline, ISD has been a long time in the making. Some experts credit the contributions of early philosophers such as Aristotle as the basis for the current philosophies of learning. Others credit psychologist Edward Thorndike, who in the 1920s promoted the stimulus-response model of behavioral psychology. B. F. Skinner, however, is considered by most to be the originator of contemporary instructional design. In 1954 he published *The Science of Learning and the Art of Teaching*, which initiated a shift away from the uninformed application of instructional technology and toward the formulation of more theoretical models of learning. The next major milestone in ISD was reached in 1956 when Benjamin Bloom, an educational psychologist at the University of Chicago, published his taxonomy of intellectual behaviors (Bloom, 1956).

In 1965 psychologist Robert Gagné extended Bloom's thinking to include nine instructional events that detail the conditions necessary for learning to occur. These events have long since been used for the basis for the design of instruction and the selection of appropriate media.

No discussion of ISD would be complete without mentioning the contributions of Donald Kirkpatrick, the father of training evaluation. In 1959 he published his theory on training evaluation in a series of articles in the *U.S. Training and Development Journal*. Subsequently these articles were incorporated into Kirkpatrick's book, *Evaluating Training Programs* (1975). His theory has now become the most widely used and popular model for the evaluation of training programs. Figure 1.1 shows a time line of the history of ISD.

FIGURE 1.1. A TIME LINE OF ISD.

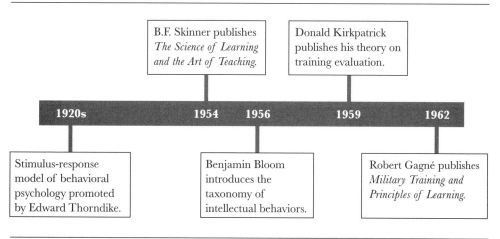

At this point some readers might be wondering why so much attention is being paid to the history of ISD and the individuals who shaped this methodology. The answer is that in order to appreciate why this approach to training development has shown an inability to communicate the value of training to businesses, one must first understand the factors and the individuals who forged the underlying philosophy of the approach.

Gagné, who was responsible for the nine steps of instruction, was an Ivy League–trained psychologist. Bloom, who contributed his taxonomy, earned a Ph.D. in education from the University of Chicago. Skinner also had a Ph.D. in psychology. In short, the training and background of the major contributors to the methodology were heavy in human behavior and education but virtually devoid of any business acumen. The backgrounds of ISD founders account for the focus and philosophy of the approach of being concerned with behavior and human performance, not business impact.

As ISD has matured, several variations of the approach have arisen, with each new approach claiming that its model is more conducive to developing effective instruction. As we shall see in the next section, each of these versions of ISD suffers from the same flaw: a lack of business tools and techniques.

ISD Models

The most basic ISD is a five-phase approach: analysis, design, development, implementation, and evaluation, referred to as the ADDIE model.

The maturation of ISD and the increased introduction of technology into training programs have led to dozens of variations to the ADDIE model. Two of the more popular are the ROPES model, developed specifically to address e-learning, and the Dick and Carey model, credited with offering cost-effective implementation and highly effective learning outcomes for the adult learners. We will look at both approaches to get an understanding of how each claims to be different or more effective yet suffers from the same flaw.

ADDIE

The ADDIE instructional design model provides a step-by-step process that helps training specialists plan and create training programs. In the analysis phase, the designer develops a clear understanding of the gaps between the desired outcomes or behaviors and the audience's existing knowledge and skills. The design phase documents specific learning objectives, assessment instruments, exercises, and content. The creation of learning materials is completed in the development phase. During implementation, these materials are delivered or distributed to the student group. After delivery, the effectiveness of the training materials is evaluated. Each phase has an objective to accomplish, activities that must take place, tools to help accomplish the objectives, and outputs that feed into the next phase.

The five phases of ADDIE essentially answer these questions:

1. What needs to be learned?
2. How should we teach it?
3. Does our prototype match our design?
4. Was the class attended?
5. Was the training accomplished?

Figure 1.2 shows the questions that ADDIE answers.

FIGURE 1.2. WHAT ADDIE ANSWERS.

A **Analyze**
       What needs to be learned?

D **Design**
       How should we teach it?

D **Develop**
       Does our prototype match our design?

I **Implement**
       Was the class attended?

E **Evaluate**
       Was the instruction successful?

Analyze. The objective of the analyze phase is to determine what the student needs to learn. During this phase, instructional designers typically rely on four approaches to analyze training and requirements: a training needs assessment, a job-task analysis, a learner analysis, and a context analysis. Some of the activities that take place during this phase are population analysis, task analysis, and problem identification. The designer uses surveys, task analysis forms, and population analysis forms as tools and delivers learner profiles, task analysis, and a description of constraints at the end of the phase. Figure 1.3 provides a graphical view of some of the objectives, activities, tools, and deliverables that are expected as a result of this phase.

Design. Design has been called the blueprinting stage of instructional design. The objective of this phase is to determine what needs to be learned. Instructional

FIGURE 1.3. ADDIE ANALYZE PHASE.

Objective	Activities	Tools	Deliverables
To determine what needs to be learned	Needs assessment Problem identification Task analysis Population analysis	Task analysis Population analysis Surveys	Learner profile Task analysis Description of constraints

designers identify all the specifications necessary to complete the project. They write learning objectives, develop test items, construct course content, plan or develop instructional strategies and methods, and identify resources. Some of the tools used to accomplish these activities include measurable verbs, performance agreement charts, and Bloom's taxonomy (see Figure 1.4).

FIGURE 1.4. ISD DESIGN PHASE.

Objective	Activities	Tools	Deliverables
To specify how the tasks identified in analyze are to be learned	Write objectives Develop test items Plan instruction Identify resources	Measurable verbs Performance agreement chart Bloom's taxonomy	Measurable objectives Instructional strategy Prototype specifications

Develop. The objective of the develop phase is to produce the instructional materials that will be used in the training program—for example, course materials, learning activities, lesson plans, leader's guide tests, and other assessment materials. The activities that take place include working with authors, flowcharting the course, and producing workbooks. Training development is no longer limited to print materials and stand-up training in a classroom; instructional designers now must consider producing audio, video, computer-based, and Web-based course materials using computer platforms, distance learning networks, intranets, the Internet, and a host of other delivery options. The tools used in this phase include authoring tools, multimedia tools, and word processors. Some outputs might be the actual workbooks and exercises. In the case of e-delivery, the outputs might include storyboards or completed electronic courses. Figure 1.5 shows the objectives, activities, tools, and deliverables of this phase of ISD.

FIGURE 1.5.　ISD DEVELOP PHASE.

Objective	Activities	Tools	Deliverables
To author and produce instructional materials	Work with producers Develop workbooks Flowchart program Author content	Authoring tools Word processor Multimedia tools	Storyboard Script Exercises Computer-assisted instruction

Implement. In the implement phase, the course is installed into a real-world environment. Some of the activities that take place might include pilot tests and revisions, full-scale production, or train-the-trainer or even full-scale delivery. There are a variety of management tools that assist with this endeavor. The outputs of this phase include student data, assessment scores, and survey feedback (Figure 1.6).

FIGURE 1.6. ISD IMPLEMENT PHASE.

Objective	Activities	Tools	Deliverables
To install the project in the real-world context	Teacher training Pilots	Management systems	Student comments Test data

Evaluate. As an official process, evaluation is the last phase in the ADDIE model. Although many instructional designers are proponents of iterative evaluation, the tactic formally takes place only at the end. Two types of evaluation may be done: formative and summative. *Formative evaluation* refers to assessments of the instruction process that are designed to improve it. *Summative evaluation* refers to assessments of the impact of instruction, which are designed to determine whether training programs have achieved their objectives. The deliverables from this phase include a formal project report as well as recommendations (Figure 1.7).

What's Wrong with ADDIE? A glance at the phases of the ADDIE process and a quick review of the desired outcome of each show an emphasis on identifying learning requirements, creating measurable learning objectives, designing learning activities that ensure students master the objectives, and then measuring to see if the students have met the course objectives. The overwhelming strength of ADDIE is its ability to create sound instruction. As an approach to training development, the methodology is robust with tools and activities that address instruction. In terms of business objectives, outcomes, and deliverables and its ability to identify business problems, however, the approach is weak. It should be clear from the review of each of the phases that the ADDIE model contains no formal business tools and has no activities dedicated to business issues. Without such tools and activities, it is impossible to develop training programs that address business issues.

FIGURE 1.7. ISD EVALUATE PHASE.

Objective	Activities	Tools	Deliverables
To determine the adequacy of the instruction	Record time data Interpret test results Survey graduates Revise activities	Level 1 evaluations Assessments Surveys	Recommendations Project report Revised prototype

Note: Level I Evaluations refer to the measurement of reaction as proposed by Dr. Kirkpatrick.

ROPES

ROPES is an acronym for the first letters of each step in the development model: relate, overview, present, exercise, and summarize. This methodology, which was jointly developed by Jim Moshinskie of Baylor University and the Vuepoint Corporation, supports the development of e-learning courses.

Relate. The purpose of this step is to relate the new material to the trainees so they will begin to think how the topic will integrate, or mix, with other material they already know. Cognitive psychologists say that this relating procedure, called advance organizers, is necessary because it helps the trainees piece everything together into a united whole.

Overview. This module overview has three specific functions: present the objective of the module, give the agenda for the module, and tell why the module is important.

Present. The information is presented to the learners by chunking the content into separate lessons. The new knowledge, skills, and attitudes that students need to acquire are presented here.

Exercise. In this step, trainees explore, practice, and interact with the material covered in each topic or lesson. They become active participants in the instruction.

Summarize. The final step is to summarize the module. After the learner finishes all of the lessons in a module, a summary of the content is presented.

What's Wrong with ROPES? ROPES focuses exclusively on how to deliver instruction. From the perspective of a cognitive scientist, it is a sound approach to training delivery based on proven principles. Some instructional designers have suggested that the entire ROPES methodology could be included as part of either the design or implement phase of ADDIE. In terms of addressing business issues, however, ROPES is even weaker than ADDIE. The approach contains no components for any type of analysis.

Dick and Carey

The Dick and Carey method of designing instruction is called the systematic design of instruction. This process, which is named for its founders Walter Dick and Lou Carey, is based on the idea that there is a predictable and reliable link between a stimulus (instructional materials) and the response that it produces in a learner (learning of the materials). This model prescribes a methodology for designing instruction based on breaking instruction down into smaller components specifically targeted on the skills and knowledge to be taught. And it supplies the appropriate conditions for the learning of these outcomes. It uses a four-step approach to training design and development: assess the needs, write the performance objectives, develop and select the appropriate instruction, and design and conduct a formative evaluation.

Phase 1: Assess Needs. This phase answers two questions: Where are we? and Where do we want to be? The designer must ascertain what learners will be able to do when they have completed the instruction and identify if the goal will require the learners to use the psychomotor, verbal, intellectual, or attitude domain. Two major activities take place in this phase:

1. Analyze the instructional goal. This is accomplished by listing all the skills needed to complete the task, including subordinate skills—in other words, task analysis.
2. Analyze the needs of the audience. This task is accomplished by identifying what factors affect the learners and is accomplished by using surveys, questionnaires, observations, and existing records to gather information.

Phase 2: Write Performance Objectives. The specific behavior skills to be learned, the conditions under which they must be performed, and the criteria for successful performance are used to develop assessment instruments. Assessments based on specific objectives are created, and then instructional strategies are developed. These strategies to achieve the terminal objective are identified, with an emphasis on Gagné's nine events of instruction (1962):

1. Gaining attention
2. Informing the learner of the objective
3. Stimulating recall of prior learning
4. Presenting the stimulus
5. Providing learner guidance
6. Eliciting performance
7. Giving feedback
8. Assessing performance
9. Enhancing retention and transfer

Phase 3: Develop and Select Instruction. In this phase, the designer produces small chunks of instructional materials that have meaning for the learner. These chunks may include interactions such as discussions, case studies, and scenarios.

Phase 4: Design and Conduct Formative Evaluation. Instructional materials are tested in one-to-one, small group, or field evaluations prior to distribution. Data from the formative evaluation are summarized and interpreted in order to identify any difficulties that learners experienced in attempting to achieve the objectives.

What's Wrong with Dick and Carey? This approach, like the other two, focuses entirely on instructional analysis, audience analysis, instructional strategies, and the evaluation of the success of those strategies. It uses the same tools and techniques as ADDIE and shares its weakness: the lack of any formal tools techniques, or approaches for identifying and solving business problems.

Summary

As a methodology for designing engaging instruction, ISD is unrivaled. As an approach for developing training programs that address business issues, however, it doesn't work because it was never intended to solve business problems. There are various versions of ISD, each claiming to be more effective at developing effective instruction, but all have the same flaw: a lack of business tools, techniques, and approaches.

This chapter provided an overview of ISD. It looked at the purpose and the history of the approach by which virtually all training programs are developed and examined the ADDIE, the ROPES, and Dick and Carey methodologies, discussing the strengths and weaknesses of each in developing sound instruction and presenting business solutions. The next chapter introduces Six Sigma, a methodology with a track record of solving business problems and with a tool kit of business tools, techniques, and approaches.

CHAPTER TWO

WHAT IS SIX SIGMA?

This chapter introduces Six Sigma, the rigorous and disciplined methodology that uses data and statistical analysis to measure and improve a company's operational performance. Six Sigma has a track record of not only identifying and quantifying business problems, but of designing solutions that solve those problems. This approach to process improvement and product development has proven time and again to have an immediate, lasting, and positive business impact on the companies that employ it.

This chapter develops a working definition of Six Sigma, provides a brief history of its philosophy, and then sets out its improvement and design methodologies. Depending on the state of a given training program, either of these approaches may be applied.

Six Sigma Defined

Six Sigma is a methodology that aligns core business processes with customer and business requirements; systematically eliminates defects from existing processes, products, and services; or designs new processes, products, and services that reliably and consistently meet customer and business requirements. It essentially boils down to an approach for quantifying how well a business is meeting stakeholder expectations and then applying tactics for ensuring that those expectations are met virtually every time (Exhibit 2.1).

EXHIBIT 2.1. A DEFINITION OF DFSS.

Six Sigma (DFSS) is the act of designing a product, process, or service resulting in an output that satisfies **both** external **customer** and internal **business** requirements.

Source: Breakthrough Management Group, (2004).

A major difference between Six Sigma and other quality programs, such as Total Quality Management (TQM), is that Six Sigma incorporates a control phase with ongoing checks in order to ensure that once improvements are achieved, they are not a one-time or temporary phenomenon, but maintained over time. Six Sigma methodology gives those who use it a structured yet flexible process to follow, a large and expanding tool set to employ, a configuration to clarify roles and responsibilities, and a governance to ensure compliance. Six Sigma can be used to improve existing processes or create a new product or process.

The "sigma" in Six Sigma is the Greek letter that statisticians use to represent the standard deviation of a population: it tells how much variability there is within a group of items (the "population"). The more variation there is, the bigger the standard deviation is. Thus, the sigma level is tied directly to the number of defects: the fewer the defects, the higher the sigma level, and the better the quality.

Each time that a process or product does not meet stakeholders' expectations, it is counted as a defect. To achieve Six Sigma, a process must not produce more than 3.4 defects per million opportunities. To put this in perspective, if you were a publisher and a misspelled word was considered a defect, 99 percent quality would mean that for every 300,000 words that were read by the customers who purchased your books, 3,000 would still be misspelled. Six Sigma strives for near perfection; therefore, reaching Six Sigma quality would mean that for the same 300,000-word opportunity, only 1 word would be misspelled. For training programs, a defect would be anything that did not meet customer requirements. It could be a misspelled word, a simulation that has incorrect information or does not work properly, a hyperlink that is broken, or a course taking too long to complete or costing too much. In short, anything that does not meet a customer requirement is considered a defect.

The Six Sigma philosophy can be captured as a methodology that allows companies to:

1. Consistently meet customer requirements
2. Use data to drive all decision making
3. Do everything with quality

In other words, Six Sigma is a customer-focused, data-driven, measurement-based strategy that allows companies to meet customer requirements virtually every time.

The History of Six Sigma

When many people think of Six Sigma, the first name that comes to mind is Jack Welch. Welch was the CEO of General Electric who championed Six Sigma and in the process made it a household word in corporate America. Welch launched the effort in late 1995 with two hundred projects and intensive training programs, moved to three thousand projects and more training in 1996, and undertook six thousand projects and still more training in 1997. The initiative was a stunning success, delivering far more benefits than Welch had first envisioned. Six Sigma delivered $320 million in productivity gains and profits, more than double Welch's original goal of $150 million.

In fact, Six Sigma greatly predates Welch and his experience at GE. A Motorola engineer, Bill Smith, is the individual credited with coining the term *Six Sigma*. In the mid-1980s, Motorola engineers decided that the traditional quality levels for measuring defects did not provide enough granularity. At that time, it was common practice to measure how many defects occurred for every 1,000 opportunities, but these engineers wanted to measure the defects per 1 million opportunities. Motorola developed this new standard and then created the methodology.

As a measurement standard, however, Six Sigma goes even further back, to Carl Frederick Gauss (1777–1855) the German mathematician who introduced the concept of the normal curve. And as a measurement standard in product variation, it dates to the 1920s when Walter Shewhart (who is credited with combining creative management thinking with statistical analysis) showed that three sigma from the mean (or average) is the point where a process requires correction.

Understanding the history of this methodology and the backgrounds of the individuals who shaped this approach sheds light on the rationale for the methodology (Figure 2.1). Shewhart spent most of his career in the Bell Telephone Laboratories, where he worked on statistical tools to examine when a corrective action must be applied to a process. Bill Smith was a Motorola engineer who introduced the statistical approach to increasing profitability by decreasing defects. The work of Jack Welch and how he turned GE around, largely as a result of adopting Six Sigma, is well documented. None of these men were just dealing purely in theory; they worked in businesses and were responsible for quantifying their contributions to the organization in a way that the business respected. As a result they understood the need to show business results.

FIGURE 2.1. SIX SIGMA TIME LINE.

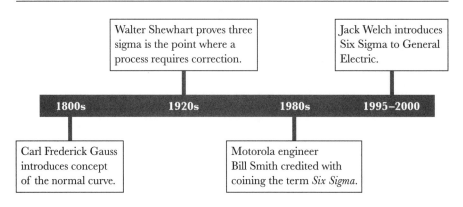

Walter Shewhart proves three sigma is the point where a process requires correction.

Jack Welch introduces Six Sigma to General Electric.

| 1800s | 1920s | 1980s | 1995–2000 |

Carl Frederick Gauss introduces concept of the normal curve.

Motorola engineer Bill Smith credited with coining the term *Six Sigma*.

Six Sigma in the Training World

Six Sigma is now being translated for effective use in human resource (HR) processes as more and more training professionals begin to see the value of this approach. The Bank of America requires project managers overseeing learning programs to apply "Six Sigma and DMAIC analytics and processes to the design, development, program management and operations of learning solutions." Home Depot expects its learning process leaders to use "Client Voice of the Customer (VOC) techniques, gain Business understanding of Learning's impact for process definition, design/redesign, improvement and maintenance of Learning processes."

At the Depository Trust & Clearing Corporation, the world's largest posttrade infrastructure organization, Six Sigma was first applied to learning programs as part of a process improvement initiative. The results were astounding: within a few months, there was a 52 percent decrease in the time required to develop e-learning programs and a corresponding decrease in development costs. Business managers who once had an adversarial relationship with the training department rapidly became partners and advocates. Buoyed by the success of the process improvement methodology: define, measure, analyze, improve, control (DMAIC), the training department adopted Design for Six Sigma (DFSS) as a development methodology. The results were even more incredible: over a three-year period, the company experienced a 392 percent increase in development productivity, a 25 percent decrease in defects, and customer satisfaction scores of 97 percent. The credibility that the customer training department gained as a result of applying Six Sigma methodology to its training programs promoted its transition from a cost center into a business unit.

Although the use of Six Sigma in the training industry is in its infancy, those who are champions of change and those who are thought leaders in the training business have already embraced it, implemented it, and are reaping the benefits.

Important Six Sigma Concepts

Three concepts are at the core of Six Sigma: the concept of the customer, a defect, and tollgate reviews. These concepts apply to Six Sigma regardless of the model and will be discussed throughout this book.

The Customer

With Six Sigma, everything begins and ends with the customer. According to iSixSigma, a customer is "one who buys or rates our process/product (in terms of requirements), and gives the final verdict on the same" (www.isixsigma.com). Motorola University teaches that there are two types of customer classifications: internal and external.

Internal customers are stakeholders, departments, and employees within the company. They are frequently referred to as *process partners*. They may use their company's products or services or may be part of the value chain that helps to produce the product. In developing a training program, a process partner might be a subject matter expert or the manager of an employee who will take the training. The requirements of internal customers are frequently referred to as the *voice of the business*.

External customers are individuals or organizations outside the company. They use or purchase a product or service in its final form and are referred to as end users. They are the reason an organization is in business. If the training group is designing a training program for the accounting department, then the accountants who are taking the training are considered the customers. Whoever is paying for the course development is also considered an external customer. The same is true if the training is being developed for individuals who do not work for the company. The requirements of external customers are referred to as the *voice of the customer*.

The same rigor that is applied to external customers needs to be applied in understanding internal customer needs. Improvements made for an internal customer ultimately lead to a quantitative improvement for the external customers.

The Six Sigma philosophy holds that these two entities, the internal and the external customers, dictate the requirements for specific products or services and thus quality (Figure 2.2). The highest level of quality means meeting the expectations of both internal and external customers.

FIGURE 2.2. INTERNAL AND EXTERNAL CUSTOMERS.

External Customer: End User/Student

Internal Customer: Process Partners

The Defect

Internal and external customers dictate the requirements for a product or service. Not meeting a requirement is considered a defect. To use a sample example from the training world, let's assume that as a training manager, you are commissioned by the accounting department to develop a program that teaches employees how to use a new accounting system. One of the requirements is that the class is no longer than one hour. You build the course, but it is one hour and ten minutes long. The course length then becomes defective. Let's assume that another requirement is that a specific logo must appear on every page of a PowerPoint presentation. Each time the logo does not appear is considered a defect. If the PowerPoint presentation is 100 pages and the logo is absent from fifteen slides, the defects per million opportunities (DPMO) would be equal to the total defects divided by the total opportunities then multiplied by 1 million:

DPMO = Total defects/total opportunities × 1,000,000.

Applying this formula to the training example would be as follows:

$$(15/100) \times 1,000,000 = 150,000 \text{ DPMO.}$$

One hundred and fifty thousand defects per million opportunities would translate into a sigma level of less than 2.5.

The number of DPMOs translates into your sigma level: the fewer defects, the higher the sigma level. The performance in the example would yield a sigma level of between 2.0 and 2.5, meaning that it would be meeting critical customer requirements (CCRs) less than 84 percent of the time.

TABLE 2.1. SIGMA LEVEL AND DPMO.

DPMO	Sigma Level	Percent Meeting CCR's
500,000	1.5	50
308,500	2.0	69.15
158,700	2.5	84.12
66,800	3.0	93.3
22,700	3.5	97.7
6,210	4.0	99.37
1,350	4.5	99.86
230	5.0	99.97
3.4	6.0	99.999

Tollgate Review

Although not unique or exclusive to the methodology that Motorola pioneered, a tollgate review is both a Six Sigma concept and a Six Sigma tool. The concept of the tollgate is common in the software development and project management worlds. In the Six Sigma universe, a tollgate review is a cross-functional review of a project that must take place at the end of each phase of the development cycle. This review is a business review, not a technical design review, and is attended by project stakeholders. There are three possible outcomes of a tollgate review:

Outcome	*Reasons*
Approval	All deliverables complete
	Move on to the next phase
Cancel	Project has low probability of success
	Customer demand has changed
On hold	Business conditions have changed

We will discuss tollgates in more detail later, but essentially a tollgate is a control that takes place across the life cycle of a project in order to ensure that the undertaking remains on target to meet business requirements. If at the end of any phase of a project, all deliverables have been met, the business review team can approve the project to move forward into the next phase. However, if, during the life cycle of the project, the customer demand has changed or the project is now seen to have a low probability of success, this team might cancel the project. The third option is to put the project on hold. This option might be exercised if the timing of the project is not right or business conditions have changed.

Six Sigma Models

Six Sigma has two major methodologies: DMAIC, which is used for product or process improvement, and Design for Six Sigma (DFSS), which is used to design or create a new product, service, or process. Both methodologies have implications in the training world. (See Table 2.2 for Six Sigma terms and concepts that are used throughout this book.)

DMAIC could be used if you have a repeatable development process that you simply want to make better. Perhaps your company is developing good training programs, but they are taking too long to get to market. You want to continue producing the same quality of programs but improve your development process so that it takes less time to get the programs into production. This example would call for the DMAIC or process improvement model. (A case study of a DMAIC project is included in Part Three of this book.)

Another perspective on applying Six Sigma to training might be that each time you create a training program, you are producing a new product; thus, each instance of a new training program being developed is similar to a new product development life cycle. Applying this point of view to training development justifies the use of a design approach or DFSS to ensure Six Sigma quality. Let's clarify the differences between these two methods by taking a walk through both processes.

The Improvement Model: DMAIC

DMAIC (pronounced duh-may-ik) is an acronym representing the five phases of the Six Sigma improvement methodology: define, measure, analyze, improve, and control (Figure 2.3). Each phase of the process forces the team to answer specific questions that are key to project success (Figure 2.4):

TABLE 2.2. SIX SIGMA TERMS AND CONCEPTS.

Term	Definition
Customer	One who buys or rates a process or product in terms of requirements and gives the final verdict on the same.
Voice of the customer (VOC)	The stated and unstated needs or requirements of the customer.
Defect	A failure to conform to customer requirements, whether or not those requirements have been articulated or specified.
Process partner	An internal customer or stakeholder; anyone in the value chain of the process or product.
Voice of the business (VOB)	The stated and unstated needs or requirements of the business or stakeholders (process partners).
Critical to quality (CTQ)	The key measurable characteristics of a product or process whose performance standards or specification limits must be met in order to satisfy the customer. They align improvement or design efforts with customer requirements.
Critical to the process (CTP)	The key measurable characteristics of a product or process whose performance standards or specification limits must be met in order to satisfy the process partners or business stakeholders.
Critical customer requirements (CCR)	A summary of the key customer issues
Black Belt	Six Sigma team leaders responsible for implementing process improvement or design projects.
Master Black Belt	Six Sigma quality experts responsible for the strategic implementations; their main responsibilities are training and mentoring of Black Belts and Green Belts.
Green Belt	An employee of an organization who has been trained on the improvement methodology of Six Sigma and will lead a process improvement or quality improvement team as part of their full-time job. Their degree of knowledge and skills associated with Six Sigma is less than that of a Black Belt.
Business review team	People who will be affected by the project or can influence it but are not directly involved with doing the project work, and can influence the outcome of the project. They ensure that the project meets business requirements.
Project champion	A senior manager who sponsors and oversees the project.

Phase	*Question*
Define	What's wrong?
Measure	How are we doing?
Analyze	Why are we not meeting customer requirements?"
Improve	What do we need to do?
Control	How can we guarantee continued success?

FIGURE 2.3. SIX SIGMA MODELS: DMAIC AND DMEDI.

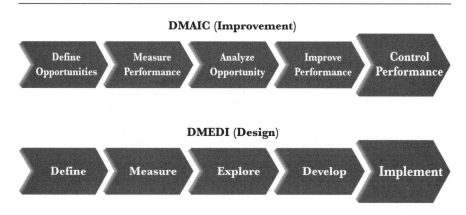

DMAIC (Improvement)

Define Opportunities → Measure Performance → Analyze Opportunity → Improve Performance → Control Performance

DMEDI (Design)

Define → Measure → Explore → Develop → Implement

FIGURE 2.4. IMPROVEMENT PROCESS QUESTIONS.

Improvement Process: DMAIC

D **Define Opportunities**
What's wrong?

M **Measure Current Performance**
How are we doing?

A **Analyze the Process**
Why are we not meeting customer requirements?

I **Improve the Process**
What do we need to do?

C **Control Performance**
How do we guarantee continued success?

Define. In the define phase, the team discovers what is important. It identifies the scope of the project, the project's goal, the customer being served by the process, the customer's measurable requirements, and the measurable requirements of the business. Some of the objectives that must be achieved in the define phase include developing or validating the project charter, identifying customer requirements, identifying and documenting the process to be improved, and completing a define tollgate. (See Figure 2.5.)

FIGURE 2.5. DMAIC DEFINE PHASE.

Objective	Activities	Tools	Deliverables
Understand the problem	Develop business case	Stakeholder analysis form	Project charter
Develop a project charter	Develop opportunity statement	Charter template	Goal statement
Identify critical-to-quality issues (CTQs)	Develop goal statement	Affinity diagram	Scope definition
	Identify project scope	Process maps	Process maps
Develop a plan to manage the project	Develop project plan		Team
	Process mapping		Critical to quality
			Define tollgate

Measure. The measure phase answers the question, "How are we doing?" The team gathers data that allow it to compare how the process is doing in relation to both the customer and business requirements. It selects what to measure, develops operational definitions, identifies data sources, prepares a data collection plan, implements the measurement process, and completes a measure tollgate. (See Figure 2.6.)

FIGURE 2.6. DMAIC MEASURE PHASE.

Objective	Activities	Tools	Deliverables
Identify key measures	Research customers	Voice of the customer	Customer's stakeholders and segmentation
Specify critical customer requirements	Identify customer and business needs	Affinity diagram	Key measures identified
Synthesize information and create output from measure	Translate needs into critical to customer and business requirements	Quality function deployment	Voice of customer
		CCR matrix	Sigma level identified
	Prioritize critical customer requirements (CCRs)	Structure tree	Product or service requirements definition
	Establish target sigma performance		CCR definition
	Complete CCR matrix		Measure tollgate
	Project review		

Analyze. In the analyze phase, the data collected during measure are fed into a variety of statistical and analytical tools in order to verify exactly what is wrong with the process. The data are then stratified and analyzed in order to identify specific problems, and the root causes of the problem are identified and validated. Thus, the question, "What's wrong?" is answered. In order to complete this phase, the team performs data analysis and process analysis and completes the analyze tollgate. (See Figure 2.7.)

Improve. The feedback from the analyze phase allows the team to begin the improve phase, where it identifies, evaluates, and selects the appropriate solutions. In this phase, the question, "What do we need to do?" is addressed. The team must generate creative solutions, refine the generated solutions, select the appropriate solutions, run a pilot, implement a full-scale solution, and complete the improve tollgate. (See Figure 2.8.)

FIGURE 2.7. DMAIC ANALYZE PHASE.

Objective	Activities	Tools	Deliverables
Understand the cause of the problem	Identify gaps between current performance and the goal performance Generate list of possible causes Prioritize list of "vital few" causes Verify and quantify the root causes of variation Determine the performance gap Display and communicate the gap/opportunity in financial terms	Statistical analysis tools Root cause analysis Regression analysis Fishbone diagram	Data analysis Process analysis Root cause analysis Opportunity Analyze tollgate

Control. Finally, the control phase of the DMAIC model puts checks and controls in place that prevent the process from reverting to its original state. The team then verifies a reduction in the root causes, develops standards and procedures, and integrates and manages the solutions into the daily work. Thus, the team validates what needs to be done to ensure ongoing quality. To complete the control phase, the team documents the improvement, establishes ongoing process measurements, builds a process management plan, and completes the control tollgate. (See Figure 2.9.)

FIGURE 2.8. DMAIC IMPROVE PHASE.

Objective	Activities	Tools	Deliverables
Select the best solutions	Process mapping	Process maps	Design implementation plan
	Cost-benefit analysis	Failure mode effects analysis	Tested solutions
	Pilot		Improve tollgate
	Implement full scale	Design of experiments	
		Process control plan	

The Design Model: DFSS

In the Breakthrough Management Group's DFSS for Transactional Environments class, DFSS is described as "the act of designing a product, process or service resulting in an output that satisfies both external customer and internal business requirements." This methodology is used when a process or product does not exist and one must be created. The definition itself indicates that the process is designed to capture the requirements of all stakeholders. This is in stark contrast to ISD, which focuses exclusively on the student and instruction. DFSS can be accomplished using any one of several variations, although two are the most common. One of these, DMADV, should be used when there is no product in existence, as when there is a need to create a new training program to support a new product rollout. This methodology aligns well with developing new courses.

DMEDI, which gained popularity because of its use at Pricewaterhouse-Coopers, is a five-phase data-intense approach to product development designed to ensure that the business and financial bottom-line numbers are met. The phases are define, measure, explore, develop, and implement. Each phase of the

FIGURE 2.9. DMAIC CONTROL PHASE.

Define ▸ Measure ▸ Analyze ▸ Improve ▸ Control

Objective	Activities	Tools	Deliverables
Document and implement a monitoring plan	Develop detailed implementation plans	Gantt chart	Control plan
Standardize the process	Develop communications plans	Process control plans	Full-scale implementation plan
Document the procedures	Transition design	Communications plan	Process owner transition plan
Transfer of ownership (project closure)	Develop process owner transition plan	Scorecard	Build and control documentation
	Develop communications plans	Rewards and recognitions	Design transition
	Complete project documentation		Team lessons learned
	Document lessons learned		Control tollgate
	Rewards and recognition		Reward and recognition
	Project review and closure		Scorecard

process forces the team to answer specific questions that are key to project success (Figure 2.10):

Phase	Question
Define	What are the business opportunities?
Measure	What targets do we need to meet?
Explore	What design will allow us to meet the targets?
Develop	Does our prototype meet design specifications?
Implement	Have we met the business requirements?

FIGURE 2.10. DMEDI QUESTION PROCESS.

Creation Process: DMEDI

D **Define Opportunities**
What are the business opportunities?

M **Measure Customer Needs**
What targets do we need to meet?

E **Explore Design Concepts**
Which design will allow us to meet the targets?

D **Develop Detailed Design**
Does our prototype meet design specifications?

I **Implement Detailed Design**
Have we met the business requirements?

Define. This phase asks, "Who is the customer, and what does the customer want?" A project team is formed, the project goals are established, and the deliverables are summarized in a project charter. The define phase also provides a preliminary list of customer and business requirements. In contrast to the define phase in DFSS and the analyze phase in ISD, the define phase of DMEDI stresses identifying all stakeholders and getting an initial understanding of what each of their expectations are. (See Figure 2.11.)

Measure. Here, the team explores the voice of the customer (VOC) in more detail and develops quantitative metrics that can be used to judge the project's suc-

FIGURE 2.11. DMEDI DEFINE PHASE.

| Define | Measure | Explore | Develop | Implement |

Objective	Activities	Tools	Deliverables
Understand the purpose and the outputs of the phase	Form stakeholder review team	Stakeholder analysis form	Project charter
	Develop business case	Charter template	Goal statement
Develop a project charter		Affinity diagram	Scope definition
	Develop opportunity statement		
Develop a multi-generational product service plan	Develop goal statement		
Develop a project plan to manage project	Identify project scope		
	Develop project plan		
	Develop multi-generational plan		

cess. For all key customer requirements, a measurement system must be in place and its validity established. The team finishes the phase by developing quantitative product requirements that reflect a balance of customer needs and business requirements. Here again, Six Sigma focuses on understanding the needs of all stakeholders. The measure phase is also when quantitative measures for all customers are established. (See Figure 2.12.)

Explore. After defining requirements, the team needs to answer the question, "What is the best way to meet our customer needs at a conceptual design level?" During this phase, the team will discover if there are conflicts between customer needs and the company's ability to meet those needs, conflicts between different design parameters, or conflicts between cost and performance. This is the phase where trade-offs or compromises are made. (See Figure 2.13.)

FIGURE 2.12. DMEDI MEASURE PHASE.

Define ▸ **Measure** ▸ Explore ▸ Develop ▸ Implement

Objective	Activities	Tools	Deliverables
Understand the purpose and outputs of measure	Research customers	Voice of the customer	Customers and stakeholders and segmentation
Understand how to develop and specify critical customer requirements (CCRs) using quality functional deployment (QFD) and other methods	Identify customer and business needs	Affinity diagram	Voice of customer
	Translate needs into critical-to-customer and business requirements	Quality function deployment	Competitive benchmarking
		CCR matrix	Product and service requirements definition
Begin QFD work for one project	Organize information using QFD matrix	Structure tree	Critical-to-customer requirements definition
Understand how to collect and use VOC and benchmarking information for design	Prioritize CCRs		
	Establish target sigma performance		
Begin work on VOC plan for one project	Complete CCR matrix		
Synthesize information and create output from the measure phase	Project review		

Develop. In the develop phase, the detailed design occurs. In addition to designing the core service, attention should be paid to developing information technology elements of the project, establishing a plan for human resources, developing sites and facilities, and purchasing materials required for implementation. As the solution is developed, the team should take advantage of lean tools to maximize speed and minimize waste in the new process. In particular, value-added analysis is beneficial to many projects. (See Figure 2.14.)

Implement. The objective of the implement phase is to conduct a successful pilot, transfer ownership of the project to the new process owner, and implement

FIGURE 2.13. DMEDI EXPLORE PHASE.

Define ▸ Measure ▸ Explore ▸ Develop ▸ Implement

Objective	Activities	Tools	Deliverables
Understand the purpose and the outputs of explore step	Translate CCRs into functions	Quality functional deployment	Product and service design concepts
Use a house of quality to deploy critical customer requirements (CCRs) to design pieces	Identify conceptual alternatives	Capability analysis	High-level production process design
	Select best-fit concept	Creativity tools	Design elements definition
	Develop functional deployment map	CCR matrix	
Use creative techniques to develop alternative concepts	Evaluate CCRs versus functions with quality functional deployment matrix	Functional deployment maps	Functional capability assessment
		Benchmarking	Performance (sigma) capability assessment
Evaluate conceptual designs	Perform functional capability assessment		Scorecard
Develop high-level designs	Translate functional requirements into high-level design elements		
Assess and select the best high-level design	Perform sigma capability assessment		
Assess the risk of the high-level design	Project review		

the new service. One of the key benefits of the Six Sigma methodology is the rigor around implementation and process control. Everyone has worked on a project that started off well only to watch it fall apart when the solution was implemented. With solid up-front work in the implement phase, these issues can be avoided.

As was the case with the improvement methodology (DMAIC) in order to accomplish the activities required in design, Six Sigma provides a wide and growing set of tools to assist users in accomplishing this.

FIGURE 2.14. DMEDI DEVELOP PHASE.

Objective	Activities	Tools	Deliverables
Understand the purpose and outputs of develop	Translate high-level design elements into detailed design elements	Quality function deployment	Detailed product or service design
Begin work on planning detailed design step activities	Develop detailed designs	FMEA	Detailed production process design
Develop a detailed product, service, or process design	Perform capability assessments	Design of experiments	Refined functional capability assessment
Refine capability predictions begun in the explore step	Revise design based on capability assessment	Structure tree	Refined performance (sigma) capability assessment
Develop process control methods for the production process	Perform failure mode effects analysis (FMEA) on design	Detailed designs	Pilot and validation plans
Develop prepilot and pilot test plans for the new product or service	Improve design based on FMEA	Process control plan	Process control plan
	Develop process control plans		Critical customer requirement scorecard
	Develop pilot and validation plans		
	Project review		

The Six Sigma Organization

Six Sigma is more than processes, phases, concepts, and tools. Six Sigma projects have an organizational structure that is designed to ensure program success. Six Sigma organizations are typically structured with seven functions and roles that must be developed, although not all of these roles are necessarily required to apply Six Sigma to the development of training programs:

FIGURE 2.15. DMEDI IMPLEMENT PHASE.

Define ▶ Measure ▶ Explore ▶ Develop ▶ Implement

Objective	Activities	Tools	Deliverables
Understand the purpose and the outputs of implement	Develop detail implementation plans	Gantt chart	Validation testing complete
Develop and execute the pilot, and analyze the results	Develop communications plans	Process control plans	Gap analysis and redesign
Develop full-scale implementation plans and transition to process owners	Transition design	Communications plan	Scale-up decision
Evaluate the design process and make improvements	Develop process owner transition plan	Scorecard	Full-scale implementation plan
	Complete project documentation	Rewards and recognitions	Process owner transition plan
	Document lessons learned		Build and control documentation
	Rewards and recognition		Design transition
	Project review and closure		Team lessons learned
			Reward and recognition
			Scorecard

Leadership group or council: A group of senior managers in the business, gathered in a forum that executes the implementation of Six Sigma into the organization

Project champions: A senior manager who is responsible for overseeing a Six Sigma project and is accountable to the leadership council for the success of the project

Implementation leader: The person responsible for managing the day-to-day rollout of the Six Sigma effort across the organization

Six Sigma coach (Master Black Belt): A Six Sigma expert who provides advice and coaching to team leaders, process owners, and champions

Team leaders: The person with the primary responsibility for the day-to-day activities of a Six Sigma project

Team members: Those who participate on the team, under the direction of the team leader; usually chosen because of their work in the area under review

Process owners: Usually the manager of the functional area under review

Shortcomings of Six Sigma

Six Sigma presents a logical and systematic approach to product creation and process improvement. Both the process improvement and the design variations have a focus on customer requirements and an expanding tool set to help achieve that end. Although this tool set has a proven record of identifying and meeting both the business and the customer requirements, it is largely based on quality, process improvement, product development, project management, and statistics. Thus, there are no Six Sigma tools that focus specifically on instruction or instructional design. This causes a dilemma for individuals who have been trained in the traditional instructional design methodology: learn a completely new methodology and adapt it to their vocation, or ignore the benefits that the tools bring and continue to develop training programs that fail to address business requirements quantitatively.

The solution, as we shall see in the next chapter, is a blending of the two methodologies ISD and Six Sigma. By combining these processes, training professionals are empowered to create programs that meet the requirements of both the business and the learner virtually every time. Training managers will at long last be able to deliver metrics that matter and free themselves of an outdated evaluation method.

Summary

Six Sigma is a customer-focused, data-driven, measurement-based strategy that allows companies to meet customer requirements virtually every time. It has two major methodologies: DMAIC, which is used for product or process improvement, and DFSS, which is used to design or create a new product service or process. Originally developed at Motorola in the mid-1980s, Six Sigma has a long track record of success with companies across a variety of industries, and it gives those who use it a structured yet flexible process to follow, a large and expanding tool set to employ, a configuration to clarify roles and responsibilities, and a governance to ensure compliance.

As more training professionals see the value of Six Sigma, they are using it as a measurement tool that can be applied to gauge the success of learning and development projects. In the next chapter, we explore why it is imperative for training professionals to abandon outdated training development and training evaluation methodologies and adopt a business approach to training development by combining Six Sigma with ISD. In taking this approach training managers will be positioned to deliver the metrics that matter and create programs whose outcomes business leaders respect.

CHAPTER THREE

REASONS FOR A SIX SIGMA METHODOLOGY

This chapter addresses why it is essential for training professionals to adopt a business model for training programs, thus combining Six Sigma and ISD. To accomplish this, we explore the concept of true return on investment (TROI), take a closer look at the shortcomings of ISD, and present the benefits of a Six Sigma approach. Finally, we introduce a model of design for Six Sigma that integrates components of ISD and is customized for developing training programs.

True Return on Investment

The concept of TROI is useful to an understanding of why it is imperative for training professionals to use a business model for developing training programs. True return on investment is a matter of perspective. In order to demonstrate and achieve it, training professionals must understand the perspective and expectations of all of their program's stakeholders. These expectations must then be quantified in the language of the stakeholder and formally agreed to. The program itself must be designed to achieve those expectations to the level or degree that was quantified. When the program is complete, the results must be presented in a language that the stakeholder understands and in manner that the stakeholders find credible. Only then can TROI be achieved.

A training manager would likely perceive a leadership program that receives high evaluation scores from students as successful. A chief financial officer who paid $1 million to build this program when it could have been purchased for $750,000 would have a different perspective. An operations manager who missed a deadline because her employees were mandated to attend this three-day training class would have yet another. Reporting student evaluation results to the CFO or program costs to the operations manager who missed her deadline would not be perceived as a return on their investment. Only when all stakeholders perceive the program as being successful has TROI been achieved.

Training programs typically have several stakeholders, including the individual or department requesting the training, those associated with developing the training and their management, the individuals paying for the training, and the students who will take the training and their management. In general, these stakeholders can be classified as either internal or external customers. The internal customers may use the training or may be part of the value chain that helps to produce the product. Their perspectives, referred to as the voice of the business (VOB), are translated into measurable targets that are considered critical business requirements (CBR). Meeting these requirements is considered critical to the process (CTP).

External customers are those who use or purchase the training; they are the reason we are in business. The perspective of this group of stakeholders is referred to as the voice of the customer (VOC). These perspectives translated into measurable targets are considered critical customer requirements (CCRs), and meeting those requirements is critical to quality (CTQ).

True return on investment therefore addresses both the VOC and the VOB. Thus, a training program has demonstrated TROI when both the CTQs and CTPs have been met. Figure 3.1 provides an example of some components that make up TROI.

FIGURE 3.1. TRUE RETURN ON INVESTMENT.

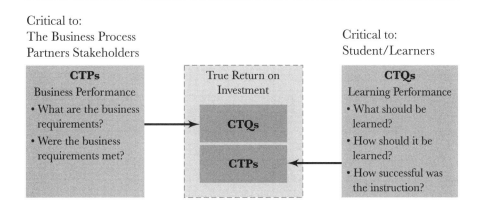

Critical to:
The Business Process
Partners Stakeholders

Critical to:
Student/Learners

CTPs
Business Performance
• What are the business requirements?
• Were the business requirements met?

True Return on Investment

CTQs

CTPs

CTQs
Learning Performance
• What should be learned?
• How should it be learned?
• How successful was the instruction?

When ISD Is Used as a Development Methodology

Let's take a look at two scenarios that typify what happens when ISD is used as a development methodology:

You are headed to a lessons-learned meeting to give a final report on a training program that your group was commissioned to develop. This program taught employees how to use a new feature of an internally developed processing system. You consider this training program to be some of your best work, and for the first time, you had the opportunity to track all of Kirkpatrick's four levels of evaluation. The level 1 appraisal showed that 99 percent of the learners felt that every aspect of the training was excellent. Every student passed the level 2 course assessment. A posttraining interview was done with students and their supervisors, and virtually everyone who attended the training was now using the new feature. As you walk out of your office to attend the meeting, your secretary hands you a report from operations: the decreased processing time saved the company $10,000 last quarter.

As you give your report, you can't understand why you are the only one smiling. You go back to your seat a little confused. The CFO acknowledges the $10,000 savings and then points out that the cost to develop and deploy the training was $160,000: it will take four years to recoup the cost of the best work you have ever done.

You are the manager of e-learning for a small financial services industry firm. One of the company's business units is about to launch a new product. The manager of the product line approaches you about developing an e-learning course to teach users how to use this new service. You engage the internal client in a discussion about what information the training should cover, time frame, system access, subject matter expert (SME) issues, and system specifications. You explain the value of evaluations and posttraining follow-up. You also convince the product manager that tracking product use once the training is completed will demonstrate the business impact of training. Finally you describe how the training can be hosted on the company's learning management system (LMS), which will track who has taken the training and generate reports that demonstrate how much students learned by taking the course, how long students were online, and how many times they visited the training.

Everyone is excited about the project. The product manager is impressed with the methods that you are going to employ to ensure that the training really worked. You are ecstatic because you finally have someone from the business unit who understands the importance of tracking and measuring training impact. The two of you agree that you will put together a project plan and that the work should begin right away.

You go back to your office to begin work on the project plan when you receive a call. The product manager (still excited) says, "Just one more thing. How much is this going to cost?" You send the product manager a detailed project plan indicating the cost of each task in the process. Sensing that there may be a problem, you attach a note saying that as soon as you get the okay from him, your group will begin the work. A couple of days go by with no word from the product manager. At the end of the third day, you receive an invitation to meet with the product manager and his boss. The subject line in the request is "training costs."

At the meeting, you give the product manager and his boss a detailed description of the costs associated with each phase of the project. You even identify ways that you can reduce the overall cost by about 10 percent. The meeting ends with an agreement that the product manager will contact you within a couple of days on how they would like to proceed.

Another week goes by with no word from the product manager. Your follow-up e-mail goes unanswered. You leave a voice mail message before heading home for the weekend. When you arrive at work on Monday morning, there is an e-mail from the product manager informing you that the division has decided not to use e-learning with this release of the product but will contact you if there turns out to be a future need. Later that day, you run into the product manager at a company function. You pull her aside and ask what happened. Her reply is, "Listen, all we wanted was a brief overview highlighting that our new service was available. All of this level 1 stuff, follow-up, and tracking sounds good, but there's no way we're spending that type of money just to let people know that the product is available. You training folks just don't understand real business."

In neither of these scenarios was TROI established. The end result in each was a dissatisfied customer who had the impression that the training group either did not truly understand or was unable to meet the business requirements. In both cases, there was a genuine attempt on the part of the training manager to show the business impact of training, but the manager used a training methodology, not a business methodology, to address the issues. If training professionals are to consistently develop training programs that solve business problems, deliver a quantifiable return on investment, and justify the existence of the training department, they cannot use ISD alone.

Shortcomings of ISD

Even a cursory examination of ISD sheds immediate light on why programs designed using this methodology have difficulty showing business impact. Table 3.1 gives an overview of the sample tasks and sample outputs that come out of ADDIE, the most popular version of ISD.

It should be clear that none of the five phases of ISD (ADDIE), in purpose, tasks, or outputs, address business requirements. The analysis phase addresses

TABLE 3.1. INSTRUCTIONAL SYSTEM DESIGN PROCESS.

	Sample Tasks	Sample Output
Analysis: The process of determining what is to be learned	Needs assessment Problem identification Task analysis	Learner profile Description of constraints Needs, problem statement Task analysis
Design: The process of specifying how it is to be learned	Write objectives Develop test items Plan instruction Identify resources	Measurable objectives Instructional strategy Prototype specifications
Development: The process of authoring and producing material	Work with producers Develop workbook, flowchart, program	Storyboard Script Exercises Computer-assisted instruction
Implementation: The process of installing the project in a real-world context	Teacher training Tryout	Student comments, data
Evaluation: The process of determining the adequacy of the instruction	Record time data Interpret test results Survey graduates Revise activities	Recommendations Project report Revised prototype

what needs to be learned and the design phase how it is to be learned; there is no mention of business. The development and implementation phases are where this learning product, conceived without business input, is developed and put into production. Finally, the evaluation phase is dedicated to assessing the adequacy of the instruction, but with no analysis of business impact. Figure 3.2 provides a graphical view showing that ISD addresses learning issues, not business issues. It almost exclusively addresses the issues that are critical to learners or learning performance with virtually no attention focused on business performance, and thus there is no TROI.

Evaluation in ISD

Chapter One referred to Donald Kirkpatrick and his contribution to ISD. Kirkpatrick's work dealt with the evaluation of training programs, so it is not truly a part of the ISD methodology. His approach to training evaluation, however, is the most widely used and popular model for the evaluation of training programs and

FIGURE 3.2. WHAT ISD ADDRESSES.

Critical to:
The Business Process
Partners Stakeholders

Critical to:
Student/Learners

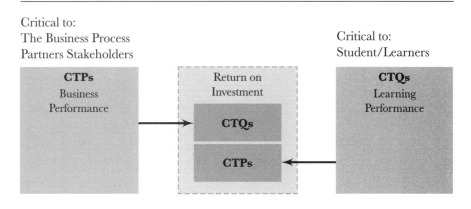

is considered an industry standard across the HR and training communities. The model has four levels of evaluation:

Level 1: Student reaction, that is, what the student thought and felt about the training

Level 2: Learning—the resulting increase in knowledge or capability

Level 3: Behavior—the extent of behavior and capability improvement and implementation and application

Level 4: Results—the effects on the business or environment resulting from the trainee's performance

Table 3.2 shows the feedback provider in this approach.

TABLE 3.2. KIRKPATRICK METHOD OF EVALUATING TRAINING PROGRAMS.

Evaluation Level	Feedback Provider
Level 1	Student
Level 2	Student
Level 3	Student or supervisor
Level 4	Training department

What's Wrong with the Kirkpatrick Approach?

None of the four levels of evaluation in the Kirkpatrick model capture business feedback or business reaction to the training product. Level I captures the reaction of the student. Level II tests the student and assesses if the student has learned as a result of the training. The provider of the feedback is the student. Level III attempts to determine if the student is applying this new-found skill or knowledge in the workplace. This is accomplished by interviewing either the student or the supervisor. Level IV, which is where the impact that the training product has on the business is supposed to be identified, is contingent on an analysis of the data collected in the first three levels, none of which even attempt to capture the voice of the business. The provider of feedback for level IV tends to be the training department or the training manager who frequently attempts to derive a correlation between the results of the first three levels of evaluation and business impact.

The Kirkpatrick Assumption

Kirkpatrick's model, which has been in existence since 1956, is based on a logical, but flawed, assertion, which I refer to as the Kirkpatrick assumption. The Kirkpatrick assumption supposes that good instruction translates into learning, which in turn causes a change in the student's behavior, and this change in behavior ultimately produces a positive monetary impact on the business. Although this is sound in principle, rarely in practice are organizational processes so tightly linked that the correlation proves true. It assumes, as Kirkpatrick stated in Evaluating Training Programs, that "the four levels represent a sequence of ways to evaluate programs." And that "None of the levels should be bypassed" (p. 21).

Thus, the Kirkpatrick assumption (Figure 3.3) essentially mandates what is measured and what is reported to project stakeholders. This mandate takes place regardless of the perspective or expectations of the process partners. It essentially states that regardless of the wants, needs, or desires of project stakeholders, training managers must measure and report on the reaction of the students, students must be tested, there must be a follow-up interview within some defined period after the training, and some calculation of these three measures constitutes return on investment in all cases.

A practical example of how the Kirkpatrick assumption is not necessarily pragmatic in a business environment can be illustrated by examining one common training program that most companies offer: harassment training.

When harassment training is scrutinized from a performance improvement or training perspective, its purpose is to change the behavior of employees so that they do not engage in behavior that harasses other employees. The traditional

FIGURE 3.3. THE KIRKPATRICK ASSUMPTION.

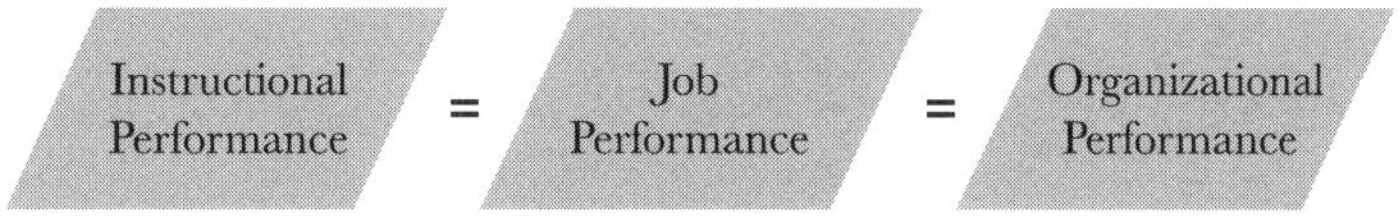

Instructional Performance = Job Performance = Organizational Performance

Good instruction translates into a change in behavior, which translates into return on investment.

training model calls for some type of survey or evaluation to be completed by students once they have finished the course. This survey evaluates each learner's reaction to the training. Some type of criterion-referenced exam follows the evaluation. The exam attempts to determine if the participant learned anything while attending the training (this is level II). Six weeks to six months later, either some type of follow-up communication with the student's supervisor or an observation of the student in his or her work environment should occur. The purpose of this observation is to determine if the student's behavior has changed as a result of the training (this is level II). Finally, six months to two years after the training, some comparison between the number of complaints or legal action taken against the company prior to the training and after the training is recommended. Performance improvement evangelists believe that the cost associated with this type of analysis is required if the business truly wants to measure the effectiveness of the training program. From a training point of view, the program is considered successful if scores on the postclass evaluations are favorable and scores on level II exams are high.

If during the follow-up communication it is identified that the behavior of the students has not changed, training professionals will quickly point out that it is the responsibility of the line manager to ensure behavior in the workplace. If the number of claims levied against the company increases, training managers will counter that there are other factors that affect the number of harassment complaints against a company. If the results of these measures are positive, the training organization will claim responsibility for the company's savings.

Examining this same program from a business point of view paints a different picture of the purpose of harassment training and sheds a different perspective on what the training program must accomplish to be successful. According to the director of labor law for one global firm, "The business rationale for offering harassment training is to limit the company's financial exposure. If we have a written policy and an audit trail showing that we provided training to all employees, it's harder for them to get money from us if they sue. The sooner everyone is trained, the sooner we're protected."

In this case, the business is not concerned with test scores. It is not important how the students feel about the course. Even the employee behavior months later isn't a factor. In this example of the Kirkpatrick assumption gone wrong, the return on investment for the business is getting everyone trained quickly. Reporting anything else would likely frustrate an executive who is looking to get to the bottom line quickly.

The Solution

It should be obvious that the learning development and evaluation methodologies currently in use are not equipped with the tools required to capture and measure business requirements. ISD, as the name implies, contains tools, techniques, and methodologies that do a good job of identifying instructional requirements; it does not, however, contain tools and techniques to detect business needs. The Kirkpatrick method of evaluation is designed to measure the effectiveness of instruction and thus does not include tools that are vital to calculating business impact.

If training professionals are to accomplish what the profession's think tanks have identified as vital to its future success and change the perceptions of business executives, business tools, techniques, and methodologies must be applied to the development process. These tools must allow them to identify the issues that are important to their business stakeholders (CTP) as well as the issues that are important to the students taking their courses (CTQ). Both the VOC and VOB must be converted into quantifiable measures. The program must be designed to meet those measures, which become the basis for what is measured and reported to stakeholders. This can be accomplished only by integrating Six Sigma into the training development process.

Benefits of a Six Sigma Approach

With Six Sigma, everything begins and ends with the customer or stakeholder. One of the first actions that occurs in this process is customer identification. Once all of the customers or stakeholders have been identified, work takes place to find out, from their perspective and in their language, what their requirements are. Once the customers' requirements have been identified, they are validated, prioritized, and quantified. These quantified requirements then become the design specifications and outcome requirements for the training program. The success or failure of the program is based on whether the approved and agreed-on design specifications and program outcomes are met. In some cases, the required outcomes may well be target scores on student evaluations. In other cases, it might be test scores, or course completion, or program cost. The learning manager, however, is not locked into an inflexible measurement model. Because Six Sigma recognizes that different stakeholders are likely to have different measures of success, the Six Sigma tool set uses various types of reporting, both quantitative and qualitative. Figure 3.4 provides a model of how Six Sigma accounts for the perspective of all process stakeholders.

FIGURE 3.4. THE SIX SIGMA MODEL.

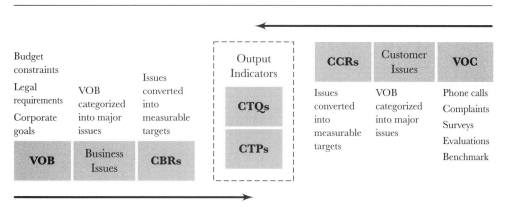

Note: VOB = voice of the business; CBR = critical business requirements; CTP = critical to the process; VOC = voice of the customer; CCR = critical customer requirement; CTQ = critical to quality.

This model represents a tremendous paradigm shift for training professionals, from a perspective where the training professional determines what to measure, how it should be measured, and what should be reported to one where those decisions are driven by the process stakeholders.

Determining Which Six Sigma Model to Use

Each time a new training program is sanctioned, the designer is in fact creating a new product. This truism makes the development of training programs perfect candidates for the creation methodology. One variation of Design for Six Sigma that is customized for training programs and beginning to gain popularity with training professionals is called DMADDI, an acronym for a six-phase approach: design, measure, analyze, design, develop, and implement. DMADDI has been called the best of both worlds because of its integration of the Six Sigma and ISD tool set. The chapters in Part Two discuss DMADDI in detail.

Summary

This chapter explored the business rationale for adopting a Six Sigma approach to developing training programs. It examined the shortcomings of the ISD and explained the benefits of a business approach to training development. Finally, it introduced a variation of DFSS, called DMADDI, as a new development model for training programs. The chapters in Part Two focus on this and explore the tools and techniques that ensure training programs meet business requirements.

PART TWO

DMADDI

CHAPTER FOUR

A DMADDI OVERVIEW

DMADDI is a Six Sigma model that has been called the best of both worlds. In this iteration of Six Sigma, Design for Six Sigma (DFSS) and ISD are combined. The tools and techniques of Six Sigma that have proven successful at identifying business requirements are employed to identify and quantify the VOC and the VOB; and the tools, techniques, and methodologies of ISD that are designed to identify learning objectives and instructional techniques are used for that end. The result is a methodology that can be applied to the development of training programs that will have the desired measurable impact on all process stakeholders.

This chapter presents a general overview of this Six Sigma derivative and explains the steps in the DMADDI process.

The DMADDI Model

The DMADDI model has six phases: define, measure, analyze, design, develop, and implement. Completing these phases in the course of developing a training program answers these questions:

What are the business opportunities?

What business targets do we need to meet?

What needs to be learned?

How should we teach it?

Does our prototype match our design?

Did the implementation meet business and instructional requirements?

The rest of the chapters in Part Two walk through each of the six phases and look at the specific tools and techniques that can be employed in each. For now, however, this chapter provides a brief description of what happens at each phase of the process (Figure 4.1).

FIGURE 4.1. DMADDI ROAD MAP.

Define — What are the business requirements?

Measure — What targets do we need to meet?

Analyze — What needs to be learned?

Design — How should we teach it?

Develop — Does our prototype match our design?

Implement — Did the implementation meet business and instructional requirements?

Define

The define phase answers the question, "What are the business opportunities?" One of the first activities that takes place in this phase is to assemble a business review team. This team, made up of project stakeholders, serves as a steering committee for the life cycle of the project. These stakeholders validate the business requirements of the project and meet at the end of every project phase to ensure that the project is on target to meet those requirements. This approach is quite different from the analyze phase of ISD, where the bulk of the activities of the phase focus on what needs to be learned. The define phase of DMADDI, in contrast, focuses exclusively on business requirements. During this phase, there is no discussion of course content (unless specific content is a business requirement) or instructional strategies. The business review team focuses exclusively on clarifying the required business outcomes of the training.

Imagine that a new government regulation requires your company to show that it has provided training for the entire accounting division on a new accounting system. Failure to comply with the government regulations will result in fines for the company. While the business driver of the training might be the government regulation, each of the business stakeholders may have his or her own perspective on what constitutes "business effectiveness." (How many times has a training manager delivered a program that addressed the "business driver" yet still had the program perceived as not affecting the business?) Only by bringing the business stakeholders together and getting formal and documented agreement on the business success criteria for the training can we avoid this phenomenon.

In this case, the business review team would validate the requirements of all of the business stakeholders, formalize the project's goals, and set the tone for the entire project life cycle. Before completing this phase, the team would undergo a tollgate review to validate that they got it right. The project would not move on until this validation occurred. (See Figure 4.2.)

FIGURE 4.2. DMADDI DEFINE ACTIVITIES.

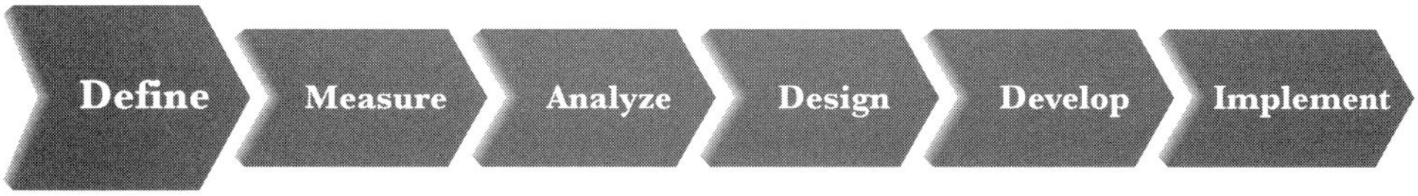

| Define | Measure | Analyze | Design | Develop | Implement |

Objective	Activities	Tools	Deliverables
Form business review team	Stakeholder analysis	Stakeholder analysis form	Stakeholder review team
Develop project charter	Develop business case	Project charter	Project charter
	Develop opportunity statement	Opportunity statement worksheet	Define tollgate
	Develop goal statement	Project plan worksheet	

Measure

The measure phase answers the question, "What targets do we need to meet?" This phase is where the business targets are identified by the business review team. Specific Six Sigma tools are used to convert the desires of business stakeholders into quantifiable targets. When this phase is complete, a tollgate review is used to validate that the business targets agree with the business case approved in the define phase.

In the case of the accounting system training, the define phase identified the business goals. Now the team verifies specific business targets. For example, in the define phase, it might have been identified that the training must be completed "fast" or "ASAP." The measure phase quantifies what "fast" or "ASAP" means—whether it is two months, six weeks, or one year, for example. The team must ensure that each business requirement has a measurable target. The measure phase is not complete until the team completes a tollgate review that validates that the measurable targets identified in the phase do not contradict the outcomes that were agreed to in the define phase. (See Figure 4.3.)

FIGURE 4.3. DMADDI MEASURE ACTIVITIES.

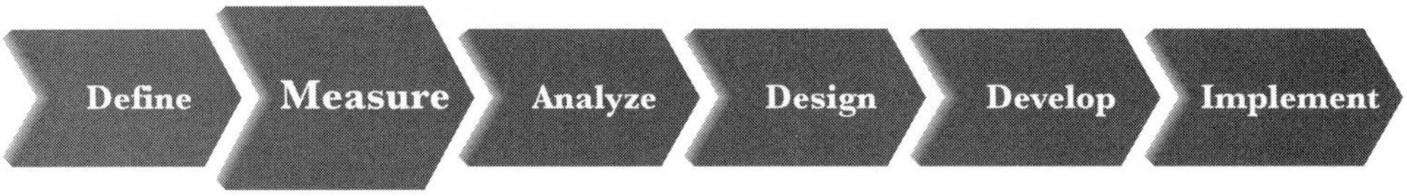

| Define | Measure | Analyze | Design | Develop | Implement |

Objective	Activities	Tools	Deliverables
To identify measurable business targets	Identify business requirements Prioritize and categorize business requirements Translate requirements into measurable targets	Affinity Analytical hierarchy process Quality functional deployment Requirements analysis	Critical-to-customer requirements definition Measure tollgate

Analyze

"What needs to be learned?" is the question that the analyze phase addresses. This phase occurs much as it would with ISD, but with a few exceptions. A combination of Six Sigma and ISD tools is used to validate the topics that the course needs to cover. The work that occurs now is accomplished not by the business review team but by the project team that will be designing the training. At the end of this phase, the project team presents its findings to the business review team at a toll-gate review to ensure that the outcomes complement what was agreed to in the define and measure phases. If the business review team finds that the outputs contradict what was agreed to in the define and measure phases, they can put the project on hold and assess if the project scope needs to be redefined or the analysis redone. In any event, the tollgate review ensures that the project does not deviate from the agreed-on scope. (See Figure 4.4.)

FIGURE 4.4. DMADDI ANALYZE ACTIVITIES.

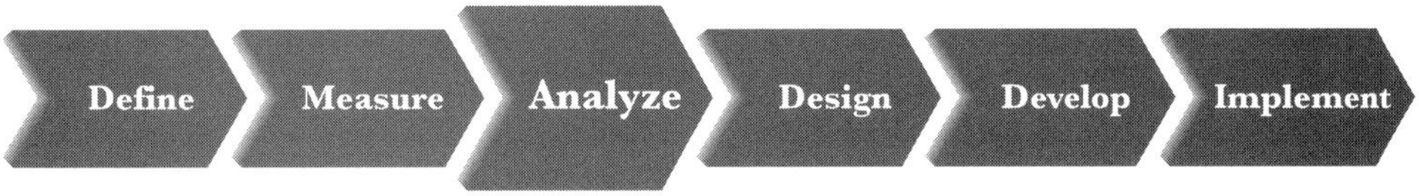

| Define | Measure | **Analyze** | Design | Develop | Implement |

Objective	Activities	Tools	Deliverables
To determine what needs to be learned	Needs assessment	Task analysis	Learner profile
	Problem identification	Population analysis	Task analysis
	Task analysis	Surveys	Description of constraints
	Population analysis	Fishbone diagrams	Quantifiable learning requirements
		Affinity diagrams	Analyze tollgate

Design

The design phase answers the question, "How should we teach it?" As was the case with the analyze phase, this work is accomplished by the project team. This crucial phase is where the instructional techniques, delivery mechanisms, activities, and exercises are put in place. At its conclusion, the project team must again present its findings to the business review team at a tollgate review. The project continues only if the outputs of the phase align with the outputs of the previous phases. (See Figure 4.5.)

FIGURE 4.5. DMADDI DESIGN ACTIVITIES.

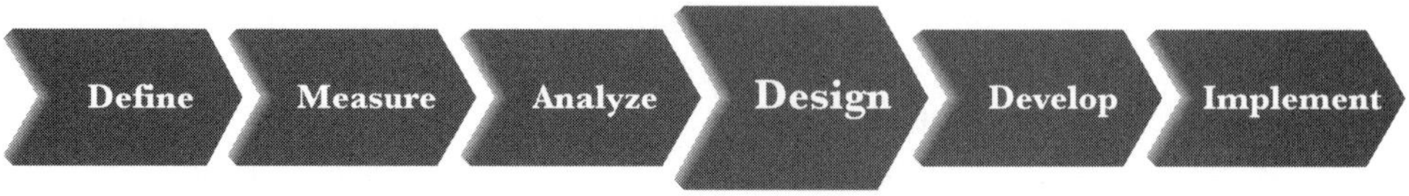

| Define | Measure | Analyze | Design | Develop | Implement |

Objective	Activities	Tools	Deliverables
To specify how the tasks identified in analyze are to be learned	Write objectives Develop test items Plan instruction Identify resources	Measurable verbs Performance agreement chart Bloom's taxonomy	Measurable objectives Instructional strategy Prototype specifications Design tollgate

Develop

"Does our prototype match our design?" is validated in this phase as the training program is constructed. Materials are created, for example, and the course is authored. As was the case with the design phase, the tools associated with ISD are primarily used here. At the tollgate, the business review team ensures that the prototype developed matches the design phase. (See Figure 4.6.)

Implement

In the implement phase, the program is installed in a real-world environment. Then the business review team validates that the program has met both the business and instructional requirements. Since there have been ongoing formal evaluations at the end of every phase, the outcome should be a forgone conclusion. As was the case with the previous phases of the process, the implement phase is not complete until a tollgate review is accomplished. (See Figure 4.7.)

Tollgate Reviews

A tollgate review is a cross-functional review of a project that must take place at the end of each phase of the development cycle. This is a business review, not a technical design review, and is attended by project stakeholders. This important concept and tool is key in the DMADDI process. At the end of each phase of the

FIGURE 4.6. DMADDI DEVELOP ACTIVITIES.

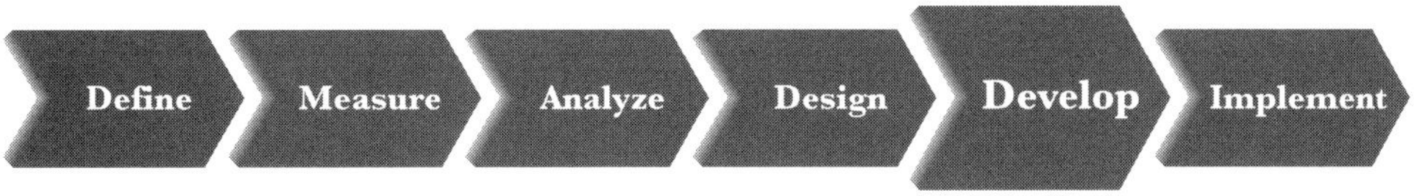

Define Measure Analyze Design Develop Implement

Objective	Activities	Tools	Deliverables
To author and produce instructional materials	Work with producers Develop workbooks Flowchart program Author content	Authoring tools Word processor Multimedia tools	Storyboard Script Exercises Computer-assisted instruction Develop tollgate

FIGURE 4.7. DMADDI IMPLEMENT ACTIVITIES.

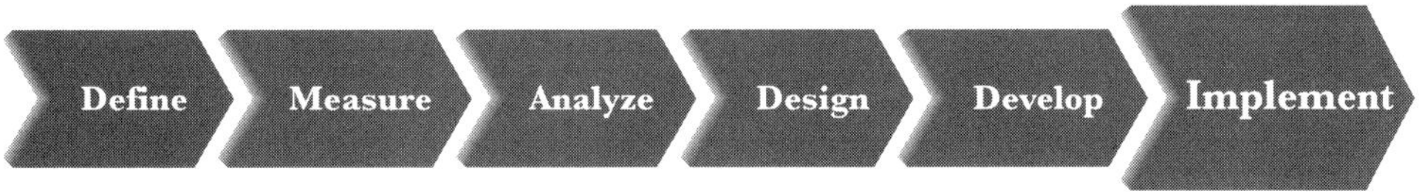

Define Measure Analyze Design Develop Implement

Objective	Activities	Tools	Deliverables
To install the project in the real-world context	Teacher training Pilots	Management systems	Student comments Test data Implement tollgate

process, a tollgate review must take place. This review validates if the program is on target to address business requirements, puts a stop to projects that have no chance of meeting business needs, and provides the opportunity to make adjustments on projects that have lost their way. It takes discipline and commitment to continually do tollgates. The rewards, however, are well worthwhile because these reviews are essential in ensuring project compliance to business requirements. Figure 4.8 provides another view of the DMADDI approach and how tollgate reviews are a formal component of the process and required at every phase.

FIGURE 4.8. DMADDI PROCESS.

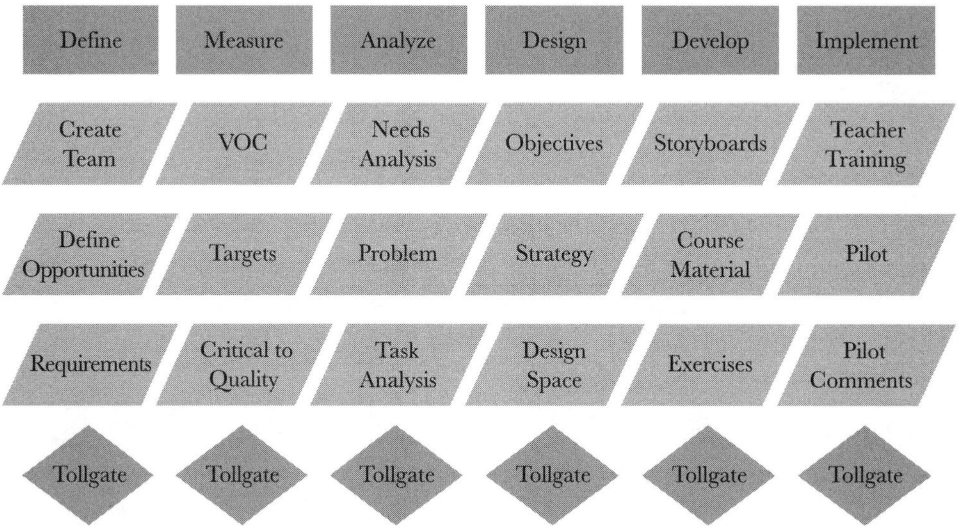

Evaluation in DMADDI

Another major difference in the DMADDI model is how evaluation is handled. In ISD, evaluation is handled as a separate activity and a separate phase. What is evaluated is dictated by the Kirkpatrick methodology. In the DMADDI model, formal evaluation takes place at the end of every phase in the form of a tollgate review. What is evaluated is determined not by Kirkpatrick but by the project stakeholders. Thus, one factor that might be evaluated in the accounting system training program mentioned previously in this chapter might be whether the program met the business requirement that it be completed ASAP. Whatever measure was agreed to about what constituted ASAP would therefore be one criterion for project success.

Project Organizational Structure

In addition to its tools, techniques, and methodologies, DMADDI provides a project organizational structure that promotes communication, accountability, and the breaking down of organizational silos (Figure 4.9). The *project champion* or *sponsor* is the person who requests the training program and thus sets the initial vision. The *business review team* sets the business requirements, determines the business targets, identifies what constitutes return on investment, and oversees the process to ensure that no decisions made will compromise the program's ability to meet business requirements. The *development team* identifies the learning requirements and is responsible for ensuring that those targets are met. The *project leader* or *Black Belt* is the glue that ties all of the stakeholders and processes together across the project life cycle.

FIGURE 4.9. DMADDI PROJECT ORGANIZATION.

DMADDI Project Organization

Project Champion/Sponsor

Project Leader

Business Review Team

Design Team

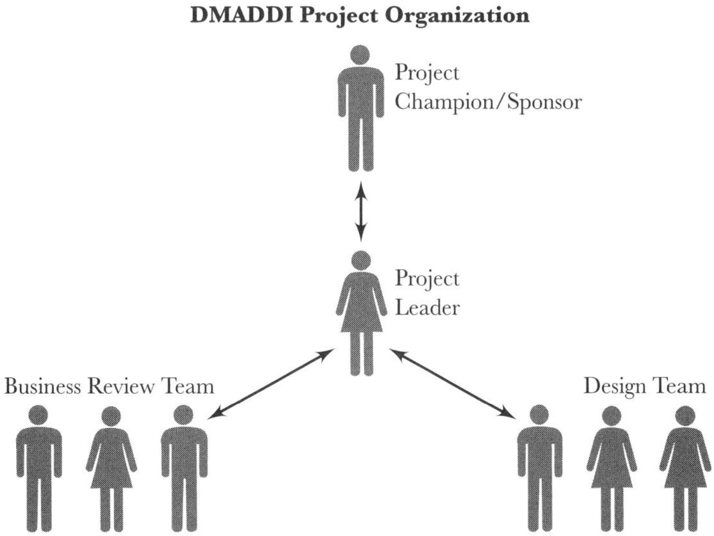

Summary

This chapter provided a general overview of DMADDI and explained the steps in the process. The following chapters in Part Two take a closer look at each phase in the DMADDI process, examining the tools and techniques as well as the inputs and outputs required in each phase. They also offer the opportunity to practice using some of the Six Sigma tools for training programs.

CHAPTER FIVE

DEFINE

What Are the Business Requirements?

Define is the first, and probably the most important, phase in the DMADDI process (Figure 5.1). If the information in this phase is incorrect, the learning project has virtually no chance of meeting business expectations. In DMADDI, the define phase is where the business requirements are flushed out. Thus, the question, "What are the business requirements?" is answered. This is accomplished as a team exercise and led by a team leader (Black Belt or Green Belt) who has been trained in using the Six Sigma tool set.

As we progress through the chapters in Part Two, we will learn the steps required to complete the define phase. We will also have the opportunity to study some of the tools and techniques that Six Sigma employs in order to ensure that the training project meets business requirements. This includes some important leadership techniques that Six Sigma professionals are trained in. These skills are essential to heading up effective teams, yet are rarely included in curriculum that teaches individuals how to be instructional designers.

Why a Separate Phase for Business Analysis?

Training professionals using ISD who attempt to identify the business requirements of a training program typically attempt this analysis during the same phase

FIGURE 5.1. DMADDI ROAD MAP: DEFINE.

Define   What are the business requirements?

Measure   What targets do we need to meet?

Analyze   What needs to be learned?

Design   How should we teach it?

Develop   Does our prototype match our design?

Implement   Did the implementation meet business and instructional requirements?

when they also seek to identify learning objectives and audience profiles and do a job analysis. This practice has proven unsuccessful for a few reasons:

- Instructional designers tend to be more interested in practicing their vocation of designing instruction.
- Identifying business requirements requires a different skill set from the skills required to create learning objectives.
- The tools available in the analysis phase of ADDIE are not equipped to capture customer requirements sufficiently.

The DMADDI methodology overcomes this deficiency by separating the business analysis of a training project from the learning analysis. In the define phase, the following objectives are achieved:

- A business review team is formed.
- A project charter is developed and validated.
- A project storyboard is created.
- A define tollgate is completed.

Completing these objectives ensures that the question, "What are the business requirements?" is answered. It also ensures that the objectives are accomplished as a result of the team's engaging in activities such as performing a stakeholder analysis, developing a business case, as well as developing opportunity and goal statements and using tools like the stakeholder analysis form, a project charter, and an opportunity statement worksheet.

The team members will know that they have been successful in this phase when they have a stakeholder review team in place and an approved project charter, and they have passed a tollgate review. Let us now take a closer look at the steps required to complete the define phase of DMADDI (Figure 5.2).

FIGURE 5.2. DMADDI DEFINE ACTIVITIES.

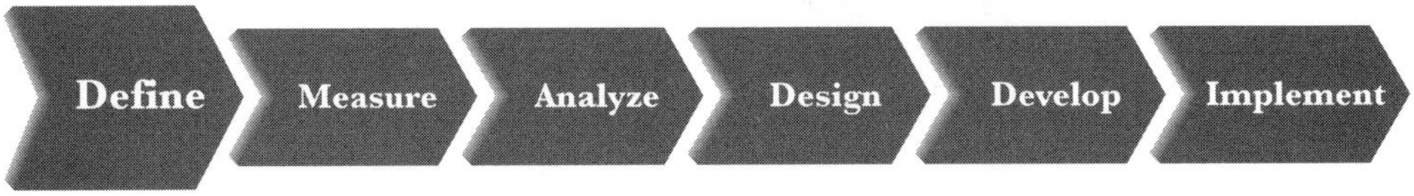

Define ▶ Measure ▶ Analyze ▶ Design ▶ Develop ▶ Implement

Objective	Activities	Tools	Deliverables
Form business review team	Stakeholder analysis	Stakeholder analysis form	Stakeholder review team
Develop project charter	Develop business case	Project charter	Project charter
	Develop opportunity statement	Opportunity statement worksheet	Define tollgate
	Develop goal statement	Project plan worksheet	

Define Step 1: Form a Business Review Team

A business (or stakeholder) review team is made up of people who will be affected by the project or can influence the project but are not directly involved in doing the project work. These individuals can influence the outcome of the project.

They tend to be those in the value chain of the training program. If the training is for employees, potential team members might be the funding source, the manager of the individuals attending the training, the managing director of an operational area, or a product manager for the product that the training is being created for. In Chapter Two we learned that the two main categories of stakeholders are internal and external (Figure 5.3). The members of the team should be as senior as possible. The more senior they are, the less likely it is that any decisions the team makes will be overturned. The project leader (a Black Belt or Green Belt) is the individual who has the responsibility of putting the stakeholder review team together.

FIGURE 5.3. CUSTOMER DEFINITIONS.

External Customer: End User/Student

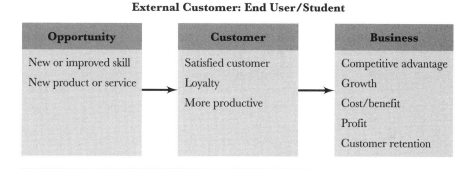

Opportunity	Customer	Business
New or improved skill	Satisfied customer	Competitive advantage
New product or service	Loyalty	Growth
	More productive	Cost/benefit
		Profit
		Customer retention

Internal Customer: Process Partners

Opportunity	Customer	Business
Improved well-being	Loyalty	Capacity
Improved product or service	Customer satisfied	Cost
	Advocate	Efficiency
		Effectiveness

The purpose of the business review team is to ensure that the project meets business requirements. In Chapter Three, we reviewed two scenarios that illustrated what happens when business stakeholders and the training department have different perceptions about what constitutes success. Having a business review team made up of key stakeholders who are setting the business requirements at the start and then validating those requirements across the life cycle of the project virtually eliminates disconnects.

Choosing the right team members is an important step. One tool that can help with the process is the stakeholder analysis form.

DMADDI Stakeholder Analysis Form

A stakeholder analysis form (Exhibit 5.1) is a matrix to fill out that helps to identify a stakeholder's relationships to the project and helps the project remain connected with individuals or groups inside and outside the organization that can influence project success. Although this tool is not unique to Six Sigma, it is included in the Six Sigma tool kit. The form can also assist in identifying what strategy might be used to involve stakeholders in the project and to keep those outside the team informed on the team's progress. One stakeholder that is automatically a member of the business review team is the project leader, who is responsible for completing the stakeholder analysis form.

Completing a stakeholder analysis form is a matter of the project leader's listing every stakeholder or potential stakeholder and then answering some brief questions about the relationship of each to the specific project. Let's look at a practical application of a stakeholder analysis form. To illustrate the use of this tool, we refer back to the example of the accounting system training in Chapter Four but with some added details.

A new government regulation requires that the company show that it has provided training for the entire accounting division (on a new accounting system). Failure to comply with the government regulations will result in fines for the company. These are the players in the project:

• CEO: The CEO wants the program completed within eight months and has informed the managing director of the division that his bonus is tied to successful completion of the training.
• Managing director: He has been informed by the CEO that his bonus is tied to the successful completion of the training. He has one hundred people in his division spread across three states.
• Accounting manager: He is aware of the new ruling, but his workload is quite heavy. He believes that his people are proficient at using the system, and he can't afford to let them take time off for training. In addition, he has a budget of only $150,000 to cover all training for the fiscal year. He also feels that he can't afford to dedicate his resources to help in the development of the training. If forced, he will assign one of his junior accountants as a subject matter expert (SME) to the project.
• Product manager: His group developed the accounting system. He believes that this proprietary product might be sold on the open market and can create a new

EXHIBIT 5.1. DMADDI STAKEHOLDER ANALYSIS FORM.

Stakeholder	Relationship to Project					Involvement Strategy					
	Is Affected by Outcome	Can Influence Outcome	Has Helpful Expertise	Provides Resources	Has Decision Authority	Meet with Regularly	Invite to Meetings	Speak with Informally	Copy on Meeting Minutes	Team Member	Other

revenue stream for the company. He is hoping that the training program provides the advertisement that will increase product use. He wants to see a flashy advertisement for his new system. The product manager is more than willing to provide resources to assist in the development of the training. In fact, he wants to assign his most technical resource.

• Accountants: They all feel that they know their jobs and that the new system is not very different from the old one. They don't know why they should be forced to attend training. They are overworked and want to spend as little time training as possible.

• Instructional designer: This designer hates programs that are not instructionally sound and can't wait to get on a project that is done the "right way."

• Training manager: This manager believes that developing training is an excellent opportunity to align his training with corporate goals. He wants to do this right. He feels that this is an excellent opportunity to measure training the way it's supposed to be measured. He plans on assigning his top instructional designer, Terry. Terry, unlike his other designers, is formally trained in ISD and has a master's degree in instructional design.

The completed stakeholder analysis form is shown in Exhibit 5.2. In this case, the product manager, while having useful expertise and providing a resource, will not necessarily be affected by the outcome of the training and does not have decision-making authority with regard to the training and thus is not a member of the business review team. The instructional designer and SME accountant are involved with doing the work and are therefore not eligible to be on the business review team. The CEO of the company has decision-making authority, can influence the project, can assign resources, and is affected by the outcome. He or she, however, is the individual sponsoring the project and therefore functioning as the project champion and is not eligible to be a business review team member.

Thus, the managing director, the accounting manager, an SME accountant, and the training manager will be selected as members of the business review team. Each of these people has decision-making authority, each is providing resources, and each can influence the outcome of the project. These individuals represent the voice of the business. The accountant does not have the same authority as the other team members but will be an end user of the training and therefore represents the voice of the customer.

Define Step 2: Develop and Validate the Project Charter

Once the business review team is assembled, it's time to put them to work. The next step in the define phase is to develop a project charter. Again, the concept of the project charter is not new or unique to Six Sigma. The purpose of the charter in DMADDI is to get everyone in agreement on what business objectives must be addressed by the training program.

EXHIBIT 5.2. COMPLETED STAKEHOLDER ANALYSIS FORM.

Stakeholder	Relationship to Project					Involvement Strategy					
	Is Affected by Outcome	Can Influence Outcome	Has Helpful Expertise	Provides Resources	Has Decision Authority	Meet with Regularly	Invite to Meetings	Speak with Informally	Copy on Meeting Minutes	Team Member	Other
CEO	X	X			X						X
Managing director	X	X		X	X				X	X	
Accounting manager	X	X	X	X	X	X		X	X	X	
Product manager			X	X					X		
Product developer			X						X		
Accountants	X		X			X		X	X	X	
Instructional designer			X			X		X	X		
Training manager		X		X	X				X	X	
SME Accountant	X	X	X					X	X		

Charter Sections

The DMADDI charter has six sections:

1. Business case
2. Goal statement
3. Opportunity statement
4. Project scope
5. Milestones
6. Business review team

The project charter is the compass that keeps any project team headed in the right direction. Developing a good project charter is not an easy task and should not be taken lightly. The business case, opportunity statement, and goal statement each take on a different twist depending on the perspective of the stakeholder. Thus, having a business review team comprising the appropriate stakeholders ensures that each of these components is looked at from the most diverse perspective. If there is agreement among the stakeholders on the project success criteria at the beginning, there is less chance that there will be dissatisfied stakeholders at the end. Table 5.1 shows what the DMADDI project charter might look like up

TABLE 5.1. DMADDI PROJECT CHARTER.

Purpose	Business case • Why should we do this?
Success criteria	Goal statement • What are our improvement objectives and targets?
Business impact	Opportunity statement • What "pain" are we experiencing? • What is wrong?
Boundaries	Project scope • What authority do we have? • What processes are we addressing? • What is not within scope?
Activities	Milestones • How are we going to get this done? • When are we going to complete the work?
Who and what	Business review team • Who are the team members? • What responsibilities will they have?

to this point. The charter is a living document and as more information is uncovered in later phases of the project, updates should be made.

Business Case. The business case describes the benefit for undertaking the project. It provides a broad definition of the issues assigned to the team and addresses the following questions:

- Does the project align with other business initiatives?
- What is the focus for the team?
- What impacts will the project have on other business units and employees?
- What benefits will be derived from this project?

Goal Statement. The goal statement defines the objective of the project in measurable terms. It should be a one- or two-sentence description of the symptoms that the project will address. The goal statement addresses these questions:

- What is the team seeking to accomplish?
- How will success be measured?
- What specific parameters will be measured?
- What are the tangible hard results?
- What are the intangible soft results?

Opportunity Statement. The opportunity statement describes why the project is being undertaken:

- What is wrong or not working?
- When and where do the problems occur?
- How extensive is the problem?
- What is the impact pain on our customers, business, or employees?

Project Scope. The project scope defines the boundaries of the project:

- What is outside the team's boundaries?
- What parts of the business are included?
- What parts of the business are not included?

Milestones. Milestones are high-level deliverables that the team expects the project to deliver, with some tentative dates assigned. The dates and deliverables are subject to change based on what is discovered in the measure and analyze phases.

Business Review Team. This section of the charter lists the names of each of the team members.

Validating the Charter

Once the team has developed the charter, it should be evaluated to ensure its effectiveness. One methodology for charter evaluation is SMART. This acronym is a checklist to ensure that the charter is effective and thorough:

Specific   Does it represent a real business problem?

Measurable   Are we able to measure the problem, establish a baseline, and set targets?

Attainable   Is the goal achievable? Is the project completion date realistic?

Relevant   Does it relate to a business objective?

Time bound   Have we set a date for completion?

In order to get a better sense of how a DMADDI charter might be evaluated, let's examine examples of both a good and poor business case, as well as good and poor goal and opportunity statements. We will evaluate each of these components based on the SMART criteria.

Evaluating the Business Case. Following is an example of a poor business case:

The director of a product area has received poor customer satisfaction scores for a software product that she delivered last year. Believing that her scores will go up if she provides training, she instructs the manager of the accounting division to provide training for his entire six-hundred-member employee base on the new accounting system. The director also requires that the training be completed within eight months and that completion of this training will weigh heavily on the bonus calculation of all stakeholders. The business review team will oversee the development of the training solution.

This is an example of a poor business case for several reasons:

• It does not address a business rationale.
• This is not a business initiative but a management mandate. The training request is not aligned with a strategic direction but a reaction to customer satisfaction scores. The low scores might or might not have any relationship to training (or the lack thereof).

- The director does not explain how the project aligns with other business initiatives.
- It gives the wrong responsibility to the business review team. The role of the team is not to develop the program but to ensure that the program addresses business mandates.
- There are no SMART goals associated with this statement.

In contrast, here is a good business case:

A major corporate initiative for the current fiscal year is to "mitigate risk by limiting financial exposure." A new federal regulation requires that companies introducing new accounting processes demonstrate that they have provided those using the system with sufficient training. The regulating authority has also mandated that this training take place within twelve months of the introduction of the new process. Failure to comply with this mandate subjects the company to up to $10 million in fines. Successful compliance eliminates this risk. The business review team will ensure that the program that is developed complies with both regulatory and corporate requirements.

This statement clearly identifies the business initiative as complying with a federal mandate to provide training for new accounting processes. It also clearly points out how it aligns with another corporate initiative: mitigating risks. It has the correct role for the business review team, which is to "ensure that the program that is developed complies with both regulatory and corporate requirements," as well as pointing out the benefits of doing the project, which is averting $10 million in fines. The business case is also written in a way that is SMART.

Evaluating a Goal Statement. The goal statement answers these questions: What is the team seeking to accomplish, how will success be measured, what specific parameters will be measured, what are the tangible hard results, and what are the intangible soft results? As was the case with the business case, these questions must be examined based on SMART criteria. We start with a poor goal statement:

> The team will develop the training program, validate that all employees have completed the course, analyze employee feedback, and ensure that students learned as a result of the training. The program will be evaluated based on the four levels of training evaluation.

This is a poor goal statement:

- It conveys the wrong understanding of what the business review team is required to accomplish. The team does not develop the training program.

- Under the DMADDI model, Kirkpatrick's four levels of evaluation are not necessarily the measure for success.
- This statement does not identify any soft or hard results.
- The statement is not written in a way that is SMART.

Now contrast the poor goal statement with this well-written one:

The business review team will identify quantifiable business targets for the project, validate and ensure compliance to business requirements across the project life cycle, and report findings to executive management at the end of each project phase. Successful oversight will eliminate the possibility of $10 million in fines.

This example is a good goal statement for a few reasons:

- It gives a clear and accurate description of what the business review team is required to accomplish: "identify quantifiable business targets for the project, validate and ensure compliance to business requirements across the project life cycle, and report findings to executive management."
- The statement is clear about the hard benefits.
- The statement is written in accordance with SMART.

Evaluating an Opportunity Statement. The opportunity statement addresses the questions: What is wrong or not working, when and where do the problems occur, how extensive is the problem, and what is the impact pain on customers, business, or employees? Let's evaluate two opportunity statements against SMART criteria, beginning with this poor opportunity statement:

The company has the opportunity to deploy a training program that adheres to all four levels of Kirkpatrick's evaluation model.

This statement does not identify what is wrong and does not identify the pain that the business is experiencing.

Here is a Good Opportunity Statement:

The company has recently deployed a new accounting software package. Federal regulations require that a training program accompany such a deployment. There is currently no such program associated with the deployment. The company is therefore subject to $10 million in fines. Compliance with the federal regulation eliminates the possibility that the company pay the associated fines for noncompliance.

This is a good opportunity statement because:

- It identifies what is wrong: there is no training program.
- It points out that the opportunity that the project holds is to prevent the company from facing $10 million in fines.

A Sample Charter

The sample charter presented in Exhibit 5.3 is a good example of a DMADDI charter that contains all of the required components. The business case is linked to a corporate initiative to "mitigate risk by limiting financial exposure." The opportunity statement points out what's wrong by stating that "[t]here is currently no training program associated with this deployment." It also points out the pain or consequences associated with the problem in quantifiable terms: "The company is subject to 10 million dollars in fines." The goal statement clearly lays out the responsibility of the business review team, which is to "identify quantifiable business targets for the project, validate and ensure compliance to business requirements (across the project lifecycle), and report findings to executive management (at the end of each project phase)." The team members are identified, the scope of the team is clearly stated, and the project milestones are identified.

Define Step 3: Complete the Define Tollgate

At this point in the project, some important work has been accomplished. A business review team has been put together. This team, which is made up of the internal and external project stakeholders, has put together a project charter that identifies the business case for undertaking the project, the goal of the project, the opportunity that the project affords, the scope of the project, and some initial milestones. The charter also clearly identifies the individuals responsible for this work. Before moving to the next phase of DMADDI, however, the team must verify that it has done all that was required of it in this phase and report their findings to the project sponsor. This validation is accomplished through a tollgate review.

EXHIBIT 5.3. SAMPLE CHARTER.

Team Charter		D M A D I

Project: 1234 | **Project Name:** New Accounting System Training Project

Business Case: A major corporate initiative for the current fiscal year is to "mitigate risk by limiting financial exposure." A new federal regulation requires that companies introducing new accounting processes demonstrate that they have provided those using the system with sufficient training. The regulating authority has also mandated that this training must take place within twelve months of the introduction of the new process. Failure to comply with this mandate subjects the company to up to $10 million in fines. Successful compliance eliminates this risk. The business review team will ensure that the program developed complies with both regulatory and corporate requirements.

Opportunity Statement: The company has recently deployed a new accounting software package. Federal regulations require that a training program accompany such a deployment. There is currently no such program associated with the deployment. The company is therefore subject to $10 million in fines. Compliance with the federal regulation eliminates the possibility that the company pay the associated fines for noncompliance.

Goal Statement: The business review team will identify quantifiable business targets for the project, validate and ensure compliance to business requirements across the project life cycle, and report findings to executive management at the end of each project phase. Successful oversight will eliminate the possibility of $10 million in fines.

Project Scope:
Process: Ensure business requirements are met
Start Point: Project begins
End Point: Project completion

Milestones

Task/Phase	Start Date	End Date	Actual End
( )	( )	( )	( )
Complete Define			
Complete Measure			
Complete Analyze			
Complete Design			
Complete Develop			
Complete Implement			

Team Members

Champion/Sponsor:	CEO
Process Owner:	Managing Dir.
Black Belt:	Project Leader
Core Member:	Accounting Mgr.
Core Member:	Accountant
Core Member:	Training Mgr.
Core Member:	

A tollgate review is a cross-functional review of a project that must take place at the end of each phase of the project life cycle. This is a business review, not a technical design review, and is attended by the project stakeholders, including, and probably most important, the project champion. This is a formal presentation attended by the entire team and should be facilitated by the project leader. Having the entire business review team at the presentation has these benefits:

- There is an opportunity for team building.
- Working together helps to break down cross-functional silos.
- All team members get exposure to a more senior level of management.

One tool that can assist in making the tollgate review a productive experience for all involved is the project storyboard. A storyboard is a series of pictures that tells the story of the project. Storyboards are usually created using some type of presentation software. There are three major purposes of the storyboard:

- To give the team an effective way to summarize and display the work being done on a project
- To let people outside the team know what's being done on a project
- To serve as a historical record for the project

Storyboards may be as simple or as complex as the team wants. Regardless of which option the team chooses, the team should look for opportunities to share the storyboard with all project stakeholders, even the ones who might not attend the tollgate review. One simple approach to creating storyboards is to create a series of slides that lists the project title, charter information, and findings to that point in the project. Exhibit 5.4 is an example of a template that might be used to prepare a storyboard.

At the end of the define phase, the following questions must be answered:

- Have members of the business review team been identified?
- Has each member of the business review team committed to the project?
- Has the team written a business case explaining the impact of the project?
- Has the team identified and agreed on a problem statement?
- Has the team prepared a goal statement?
- Has the team set initial milestones?

EXHIBIT 5.4. STORYBOARD TEMPLATE.

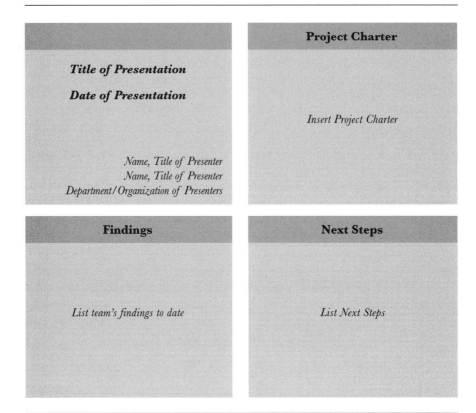

Team Leadership Skills

Teams and teamwork are essential components of the Six Sigma methodology. Team leaders in this process are required to oversee teams with members at various levels in the organization and with a variety of formal reporting lines. This can be a challenge for the Black Belt or Green Belt. The challenge is confounded when the team or project leader must also introduce new ways of tackling old problems. Perhaps the most useful tools available to individuals leading teams using any Six Sigma methodology are those associated with team leadership. That being said, teams leaders must always remember that:

- Teams are important.
- Teams come up with better ideas and solutions than individuals working alone.
- The whole is greater than the sum of individual parts.

The bulk of the work accomplished in any Six Sigma methodology stems from team interaction. Thus, it is important for individuals employing any variation of Six Sigma to be skilled in that area. The discipline of ISD and the training of instructional designers focus on teaching individuals how to develop instruction but neglect to provide these individuals with tools that can be used in the area where much of their interactions will be spent: working with teams. It is therefore important for individuals employing DMADDI to have a good understanding of team dynamics and to have the ability to lead teams effectively. Though not unique to Six Sigma, team dynamics is essential.

Team Roles and Responsibilities

Although the names may change based on the culture of an organization, all teams have four main members: the team leader, the team member, the minutes taker, and the team facilitator. The roles and responsibilities are summarized in Table 5.2.

TABLE 5.2. TEAM MEMBER ROLES AND RESPONSIBILITIES.

Member	Role	Responsibility
Team leader	Be open	Listen
	Be prepared	Be nondefensive
	Model appropriate behavior	Write down ideas
		Prepare the agenda
	Follow up	Ensure a flip chart is available
		Know the issues
		Transfer information from the team above
		Don't judge when brainstorming
		Speak last
		Be on time and end the meeting on time
		Complete assignments
		Encourage and reinforce participation
		Listen
		Volunteer to take action steps
		Review action steps from the last meeting
		Recognize completion
		If tasks are not complete, ask why
		Reinforce success and improvement
		Recognize trouble spots and solve

Continued

TABLE 5.2. TEAM MEMBER ROLES AND RESPONSIBILITIES, Cont'd.

Member	Role	Responsibility
Team member	Be open	Review agenda ahead of time
	Be prepared	Do homework to form opinions
	Participate	Add to agenda before meeting if interested
	Follow through	Bring data and copies of work to the meeting
		Listen without judgment
		Argue the other person's case before presenting your side
		Don't judge when brainstorming
		Be nondefensive
		Model the behaviors expected from others
		Be on time
		Meet commitments
		Be concise
		Listen
		Volunteer to take action steps
		Do what is committed to
		Bring data that demonstrate performance
		Let the team leader know if there is a problem meeting commitments
		Reinforce other team members when appropriate
		Participate in solving problems
Minutes taker	Be prepared	Review minutes, and complete action steps
	Listen	Review previous minutes prior to meeting
	Participate	Record major activities, decisions, and action steps during the meeting
	Be prompt	
		Ask questions if issues are not clear
		Review action steps at the end of the meeting
		Participate as a team member during meetings
		Send minutes to team leader to review
		Issue minutes to all team members in a timely fashion
Meeting facilitator	Prior to meeting	Review agenda in terms of content, time allocation, flexibility, objectives
	During meetings	
	After meetings	Discuss concerns with team leader

TABLE 5.2. TEAM MEMBER ROLES AND RESPONSIBILITIES, Cont'd.

Member	Role	Responsibility
		Discuss techniques to use (such as brainstorming)
		Tell leader what will be looked for
		Be sure there are clear objectives
		Do not actively participate unless team is off track or skipping critical steps
		If intervention is required, stay seated
		Take notes on what is observed
		Ask the team leader what went well and what could be changed
		Give positive feedback and encouragement
		Give suggestions for improvement
		Ask for discussions of points
		Summarize most critical points

Team Leader. If the role and responsibility of the team leader had to be summed up it in one sentence, the sentence would read as follows: "The team leaders must be open and prepared and should always model the appropriate behavior and follow up." Leaders of any team must listen and be nondefensive. They should know the issues, prepare meeting agendas, and make sure that the required meeting material is available. They should be on time for meetings, complete their assignments, volunteer to complete action steps, and review action steps from previous meetings.

Team Members. Team members should be willing to participate, follow through on their commitments, and be creative. Effective team members model the behaviors they expect from others. They are on time to meetings and meet their commitments. Most important, they are concise, listen, and volunteer to take action steps.

Minutes Taker. The four traits that describe an effective minutes taker are that they are prepared, they listen, they participate, and they are prompt. Taking the minutes of team meetings is an important responsibility because the minutes are the official record of what transpired and what was agreed to at the meeting. Good minute takers review meeting minutes and complete action steps. They review previous minutes prior to a meeting and record major activities, decisions, and action steps during the meeting. Effective minute takers ask questions if they are not clear on an issue, review action steps at the end of the meeting, and continue to participate as a team member during the meeting. They send minutes to team leader to review and issue minutes to all team members in a timely fashion.

Team Facilitator. The team facilitator is a highly visible role that must be filled by someone who is prepared to go the extra mile. The team facilitator does more than facilitate meetings. He or she has a variety of responsibilities that take place before, during, and after meetings. Prior to the meeting, the facilitator reviews the agenda for content, time allocation, flexibility, and objectives. The facilitator should then discuss any concerns with the team leader.

He or she should work with the team leader to come up with techniques such as brainstorming to use at the meetings. This person should tell the leader what he or she hopes will be accomplished at the meeting and seeks to ensure that there are clear objectives for it.

During the meeting the facilitator should not actively participate unless the team is off track or skipping critical steps. A facilitator who does intervene should stay seated and take notes on what is observed.

After the meeting, the facilitator should ask the team leader how he or she thought the meeting went. The facilitator should work with the team leader in order to determine what went well and what could be changed. A good facilitator gives positive feedback and encouragement, offers suggestions for improvement, asks for discussions of points, summarizes the most critical points, and is quietly proactive. The facilitator also works between formal meetings with the leader.

Planning the Meeting

Six Sigma methodologies rely heavily on the team concept. For teams to be effective and produce successful results, they must have effective meetings. One reason for poor team meetings is the lack of planning by the team leader. Failing to plan is a virtual road map for failure. It is therefore important for any team leader to be aware of and complete five steps in planning a team meeting:

1. Plan the content.
2. Decide who should attend.
3. Plan the logistics.
4. Write and publish the agenda.
5. Plan to evaluate.

Plan the Content. In order to be successful at planning the content of a meeting, the team or project lead must answer some essential questions:

- What do I want the meeting to accomplish?
- What type of techniques will I need to use during the meeting?
- Which of the team meeting purposes will be involved?

The project leader should evaluate and prepare to review the team performance versus measures, recognize any team or individual successes, and, perhaps most important, address performance problems. The leader should also plan for developing next steps from the meeting and explore ways of sharing news and information. He or she must consistently ask, "What do I want the team members to have when the meeting is over? And what will I do if the team doesn't respond?"

Decide Who Should Attend. The next challenge for the team leader is to decide who in addition to team members should attend a team meeting. The project leader may want a facilitator present to help observe or help with training or may decide that other attendees are needed. A business review team member may add value to a team meeting if the team is unclear on how a suggestion might affect a business requirement. Anyone who has something to contribute to help reach the objective might be invited to a meeting.

Plan the Logistics. The importance of the logistics of a meeting cannot and should not be underestimated. Not having a room, being forced to change rooms, or not having the proper equipment has sabotaged too many meetings. The project leader must answer these questions:

- When should the meeting occur? The leader should pick the time for the first meeting, and then the team will decide when to hold future meetings. The project leader should try not to hold meetings early Monday morning or late in the day.
- Where should the meeting be held? Meetings should take place anywhere comfortable and convenient with a minimum chance of interruptions.
- What else is needed? Is there a need for a flip chart, overhead projector, or other audiovisual equipment? Should the team arrange for lunch or other refreshments?

Write and Publish the Agenda. Once the team leader has planned the content, decided who should attend, and worked out the logistics of the meeting, he or she should then prepare and publish a meeting agenda. Without an agenda, a meeting cannot be productive. The agenda helps plan and organize the meeting, and it helps keep discussion on track. The agenda should include the following information:

- Purpose of the meeting
- Who is attending
- Starting and ending times
- Meeting place
- Topics in prioritized order
- Time allocated for each topic
- Responsibility for each topic
- Focus exercise
- Review of previous minutes and action steps
- Other business
- Summary
- Closure

Plan to Evaluate. At the end of each meeting, the leader should ask the minutes taker to review action steps generated during the meeting. This helps ensure that everyone understands the action steps and agrees to the due date for the step. The team leader should incorporate a way of evaluating the effectiveness of the meeting. Continuous improvement requires feedback on how the process is operating. Feedback using team meeting evaluations can be used to improve the meetings. A facilitator can also help improve the efficiency and effectiveness of meetings by providing feedback to both the team and team members. See Table 5.3 for a sample meeting evaluation form.

TABLE 5.3. MEETING EVALUATION FORM.

Date:		**Time of day:**					
	Never				**Always**	**Comments**	
1. Did the meeting start on time?	1	2	3	4	5		
2. Were the meeting outcomes met?	1	2	3	4	5		
3. Was the agenda followed?	1	2	3	4	5		
4. Did discussions remain focused?	1	2	3	4	5		
5. Was the facilitator adequately prepared?	1	2	3	4	5		
6. Do meetings end on time?	1	2	3	4	5		
7. Were meeting minutes received in a timely manner?	1	2	3	4	5		

TABLE 5.3. MEETING EVALUATION FORM, Cont'd.

	Never				Always	Comments
8. Were the ground rules adhered to?	1	2	3	4	5	
9. Was everyone involved?	1	2	3	4	5	

Strengths of the meeting were:

The meeting could have been improved by:

I could assist in making meetings more effective by:

The evaluation form on the following page can be given out to team members to fill out. The evaluation does not have to be done at each meeting, but should be done often enough to get feedback on what the team members think about the team's performance.

Team Leader Meeting Activities

- Initiating action
- Keeping the team on topic
- Eliciting information
- Comparing and contrasting viewpoints
- Summarizing
- Testing for decision
- Developing action plans
- Monitoring participation
- Encouraging participation
- Modeling the appropriate behavior
- Helping to resolve conflict
- Exploring reactions and feelings
- Facilitating feedback
- Managing time
- Using team skills and statistical tools

Leading Team Meetings

Once the planning is complete, it's time to conduct the meeting. A team leader balances many issues in moving the team through any series of meetings. He or she must focus the energy of the team and keep it moving toward their meeting objective; monitor progress; provide direction; analyze the situation; and determine how to move forward and take the steps to achieve the objectives. It is therefore essential that the leader be attentive to the content of the meeting, the social interaction occurring during the meeting, and the structure of the meeting.

Tips for Team Leaders

- Always start the meeting on time.
- Ignore those who come in late; do not bring them up to date.
- End on time unless the discussion is truly productive and the team agrees to continue for a specified time.
- Always say the team member's name before asking a question of him or her.
- Set clear expectations.
- Reinforce appropriate behavior.
- Extinguish or correct inappropriate behavior (in or out of the meeting).
- Use a code of conduct.

DMADDI Tools for Define

DMADDI Stakeholder Analysis Form

Purpose: To identify business review team members

When to Use

- At the beginning of the project to identify all stakeholders, isolate business review team members, and develop a communication strategy

Steps to Follow

1. Brainstorm and list anyone who might potentially be a project stakeholder.
2. Mark an X next to the statement that applies to each stakeholder.
3. Mark an X for a team member only if at least three items on the "Relationship to Project" side are checked off.
4. Discuss the results with the project champion.

EXHIBIT 5.5. STAKEHOLDER ANALYSIS FORM.

Stakeholder	Relationship to Project					Involvement Strategy					
	Is Affected by Outcome	Can Influence Outcome	Has Helpful Expertise	Provides Resources	Has Decision Authority	Meet with Regularly	Invite to Meetings	Speak with Informally	Copy on Meeting Minutes	Team Member	Other

EXHIBIT 5.6. DMADDI PROJECT CHARTER.

Team Charter		D M A D D I

Project:	**Project Name:**

Business Case:

Opportunity Statement:

Goal Statement:

Project Scope:
Process:
Start Point:
End Point:

Project Plan

Task/Phase	Start Date	End Date	Actual End
Form Team			
Finalize Charter			
Complete Measure			
Complete Analyze			
Complete Design			
Complete Project			

Team Members

Sponsor:			
Process Owner:			
Black Belt:			
Core Member:			
Core Member:			
Core Member:	TBD	TBD	TBD
Core Member:	TBD	TBD	TBD

DMADDI Charter

Purpose: To get agreement on the purpose of the project

When to Use

• After the business review team has been assembled to ensure that all perspectives are accounted for

Steps to Follow

1. As a team, reach agreement on the business case.
2. As a team, reach agreement on the goal statement.
3. As a team, reach agreement on the opportunity statement.
4. As a team, reach agreement on initial milestones.
5. Ensure that all components are SMART.

DMADDI Define Checklist

EXHIBIT 5.7. DMADDI DEFINE CHECKLIST.

Instructions: Respond appropriately to the following questions.

1. Have members of the business review team been identified?	
2. Has each member of the business review team committed to the project?	
3. Has the team written a business case explaining the impact of the project?	
4. Has the team identified and agreed to a problem statement?	
5. Has the team prepared a goal statement?	
6. Has the team set initial milestones?	

Comments:

Team Member Signatures:

Purpose: To formally end the define phase

When to Use

- At the end of the define phase to ensure that all required tasks have been accomplished

Steps to Follow

1. As a team, answer each item on the checklist.
2. Mark a question "yes" only if each team member agrees that the task has been completed.
3. Reach agreement on each answer before marking the checklist.
4. Schedule meetings to finish any incomplete task.

DMADDI Tollgate Preparation Worksheet

EXHIBIT 5.8. DMADDI TOLLGATE PREPARATION WORKSHEET.

Key Finding 1:	Supporting Data 1:	Person Responsible
Key Finding 2:	Supporting Data 2:	Person Responsible
Key Finding 3:	Supporting Data 3:	Person Responsible

EXHIBIT 5.8. DMADDI TOLLGATE PREPARATION WORKSHEET, Cont'd.

Issues:	Person Responsible
Learnings:	Person Responsible
Next Steps:	Person Responsible

Purpose: To prepare the team for the tollgate review

When to Use

- At the end of the define phase to get agreement on what will be presented to the champion

Steps to Follow

1. As a team, brainstorm a list of messages.
2. Prioritize the list of messages.
3. Agree on a sequence for the messages.
4. Agree on a supporting data.
5. Assign a resource to update the storyboard.

DMADDI Storyboard Template

Purpose: To put together the tollgate presentation for the project champion

Steps to Follow

- After the tollgate preparation worksheet has been completed phase, to get agreement on what the champion will see

Instructions

1. Assign a resource to enter information from the tollgate preparation worksheet into the presentation.
2. Circulate to the team for comments.
3. Reach agreement on contents prior to presentation.
4. Schedule practice of the presentation if necessary.

Summary

This chapter has examined the define phase of DMADDI. It explored learning how to form a stakeholder review team, developing and validating a DMADDI project charter, and completing the define tollgate. It presented some of the tools and techniques that Six Sigma employs in order to choose the right people to participate on a business review team and how to put together an effective business case, goal, and opportunity statement. Finally, it presented some important leadership techniques that are essential to heading up effective teams.

The next chapter looks at the measure phase of DMADDI. This is where the business requirements are fleshed out and the voice of the customer and voice of the business are identified, quantified, and prioritized.

CHAPTER SIX

MEASURE

What Targets Do We Need to Meet?

Measure is the phase when the business requirements are fleshed out. It is also when contention between business review team members tends to occur. This stage of DMADDI provides great opportunity for stakeholders to understand and appreciate the perspective of the other members and an occasion for the training representative to sit down with the other stakeholders and speak about nothing but the business.

During the measure phase, the voice of the customer and voice of the business are identified, quantified, and prioritized. This chapter explains how to identify business requirements, prioritize business requirements, and then translate those business requirements into measurable targets.

The Honeymoon Is Over

A couple's tenth wedding anniversary is approaching. In celebration, the husband buys her a lovely diamond ring and makes reservations at an expensive restaurant. He even rents a limousine to chauffeur them around for the night. The husband is excited, because he is sure his wife will be pleased.

The limo arrives, and the evening begins. As the night progresses, the husband begins to notice that although his wife is polite, she does not seem excited about the evening. In response, he begins to feel offended and upset. He has given his wife more than any woman could ask for. He bought her expensive jewelry, arranged for a babysitter, and has taken her out to an exclusive restaurant. What more could she want? How ungrateful!

When they return home, the husband can't contain his anger. He asks his wife why she didn't seem to enjoy the evening. The wife with love in her eyes explains that she appreciates what he did for her that evening, but she was hoping that on their tenth anniversary, they could stay at home, order pizza, and play a family game of Monopoly, just as they had on their first anniversary.

In many ways, this story sums up the relationship that training professionals have with their business stakeholders, internal and external. Like the husband, training professionals take it on themselves to determine what the stakeholder wants. Like the wife, the stakeholder politely accepts what he or she receives but is ultimately unhappy. At some point after the training service has been delivered, the training professional finds out that what he or she valued and ultimately delivered and what the customer valued and wanted were totally different. By that time, the damage has been done. The relationship is strained.

DMADDI Road Map

While the define phase set the stage and started to get the stakeholders in agreement on business requirements, the measure phase is where the business requirements are more clearly fleshed out. This phase of DMADDI makes identifying and quantifying business requirements an independent and formal part of the training development process. Thus, it answers the question, "What targets do we need to meet?" (See Figure 6.1.) If this phase is followed correctly, those in the training department will not suffer the fate of the husband who went to a lot of time and expense, only to find out that what he delivered was not what his wife wanted.

In order to answer the question, "What targets do we need to meet?" the team leader must work with the business review team to identify any business requirements other than the general goals identified during the define phase. At this point, it must be stressed that what needs to be accomplished is to identify *business* requirements, not *learning* requirements. Business requirements sound like this: "Increase productivity by 3 percent," "Decrease cost by 5 percent." They do not sound like this: "Students will be able to . . ." This separation is virtually impossible to accomplish using the traditional ISD methodology.

FIGURE 6.1. DMADDI ROAD MAP FOR MEASURE.

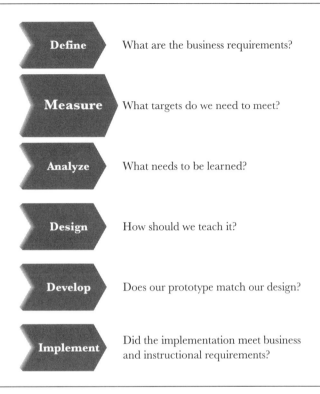

Define — What are the business requirements?

Measure — What targets do we need to meet?

Analyze — What needs to be learned?

Design — How should we teach it?

Develop — Does our prototype match our design?

Implement — Did the implementation meet business and instructional requirements?

To complete the measure phase of DMADDI, the following objectives must be achieved:

1. Identify business requirements.
2. Prioritize business requirements.
3. Translate business requirements into measurable targets.
4. Complete the measure tollgate.
5. Transfer the business requirements to the development team.

To accomplish these objectives, the business review team engages in various brainstorming activities and employs a number of Six Sigma tools, such as affinity diagrams, Pareto charts, and analytical hierarchy processes. The team will also employ combine, delete, add, modify (CDAM).

The team members will know that they have been successful in this phase when they have an agreed-on and prioritized list of measurable business requirements, have passed a tollgate review, and transferred project data to the development team. Let us now take a closer look at the steps required to complete the measure phase of DMADDI (Figure 6.2).

FIGURE 6.2. DMADDI MEASURE ACTIVITIES.

Objective	Activities	Tools	Deliverables
To identify measurable business targets	Identify business requirements Prioritize and categorize business requiremments Translate requirements into measurable targets	Affinity Analytical hierarchy process Quality functional deployment Requirements analysis	Critical-to-customer requirements definition Measure tollgate

Measure Step 1: Identifying Business Requirements

The first objective that must be accomplished in the measure phase is to identify the business requirements for the project. This can be a challenging endeavor since each member of the business review team comes to the team with a different perspective.

Sources for Fleshing Out the Business Requirements

Various sources can be used to flesh out business requirements: internal and external data, listening posts, research methods, and team collaboration (Figure 6.3).

FIGURE 6.3. METHODS OF
IDENTIFYING BUSINESS REQUIREMENTS.

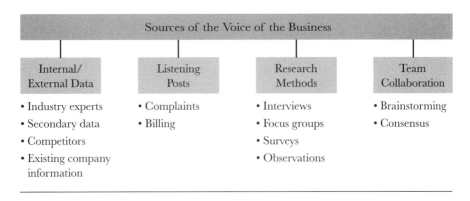

Internal and External Data. Internal and external data include gathering information from industry experts, looking at what competitors are doing, reviewing
existing company information, and examining data from secondary sources.

Listening Posts. Every company has listening posts—points of contact for customer feedback. They include the customer service desk or customer hot line
where customers call to complain. It may be the company's billing department
where customers contest bills. It could be a corporate Web site that collects customer comments. Compiling this feedback serves as a navigation system that
guides business requirements.

Research Methods. Research is a more time-consuming technique to obtain the
voice of the business. Using research as a source requires conducting customer
interviews, distributing surveys, hosting focus groups, and reviewing, as well as
spending time observing.

Team Collaboration. Team collaboration using consensus and brainstorming
with the business review team members is probably the most expedient (but not
necessarily the most accurate) method of obtaining business requirements. With
this method, we are assuming that the project stakeholders are the representatives
of their business constituency and have individually used some of the methods
described earlier to identify the requirements of their business stakeholders. Brainstorming can cause the most contention with the team members, each of who
comes to the table with a different perspective.

The scenario from Chapter Five provides a good illustration of how perspectives might clash during brainstorming. Consider again the business review team members and their perspectives:

- CEO: The CEO wants the program completed within eight months and has informed the managing director of the division that his bonus is tied to successful completion of the training.
- Managing director: He has been informed by the CEO that his bonus is tied to successful completion of the training. He has one hundred people in his division spread across three states.
- Accounting manager: He is aware of the new ruling, but his workload is quite heavy. He believes that his people are proficient at using the system, and he can't afford to let them take time off to go away for training. In addition, he has a budget of only $150,000 to cover all training for the fiscal year. He also feels that he can't afford to dedicate his resources to help in the development of the training. If forced, he will assign one of his junior accountants to the project.
- Product manager: His group developed the accounting system. He believes that this proprietary product might be sold on the open market and can create a new revenue stream for the company. He is hoping that the training program provides the advertisement that will increase product use. He wants to see a flashy advertisement for his new system. The product manager is more than willing to provide resources to assist in the development of the training. In fact, he wants to assign his most technical resource.
- Accountants: They all feel that they know their jobs and that the new system is not very different from the old one. They don't know why they should be forced to attend training. They are overworked and want to spend as little time training as possible.
- Training manager: This manager believes that developing training is an excellent opportunity to align his training with corporate goals. He wants to do this right. He feels that this is an excellent opportunity to measure training the way it's supposed to be measured. He plans on assigning his top instructional designer, Terry. Terry, unlike his other designers, is formally trained in ISD.

As you can see by reviewing these individual perspectives, each of the business review team members is looking at this project differently. The CEO (although not a team member) is concerned with time and being fined. He just wants the project completed within eight months. The managing director wants to ensure that he gets his bonus. The accounting manager doesn't want the training at all and certainly doesn't want to pay for it. The accountants also don't want the training; if they are forced to do it, they want to spend as little time as possible doing it. The training manager seems concerned with being able to tie his department's work with a high-profile corporate initiative. He also wants to use the formal ISD methodology to develop and measure training success.

Brainstorming Tools

The Six Sigma tool set contains several brainstorming tools that, if used correctly, can greatly reduce and even eliminate friction between team members at this point: the random word technique, the wishful thinking technique, the random picture technique, and the affinity diagram technique.

Random Word Technique. With this technique, the team uses a random word to generate new ideas. Using a random word as a prompt forces the team to attack the problem from a direction that is different from usual. To use this technique, the team members take a word from a random word generator such as a dictionary or book, and then extract its underlying principles and apply them to the problem. The first requirement therefore is the random word. The word chosen is classed as the initial stimulus. Next, the facilitator establishes a *bridging idea,* which is an idea based on the stimulus. This is used, as the name implies, as a bridge between the stimulus and any idea generated. Here are two examples:

> *Example 1:* The random word is *balloon.* The accounting manager might bridge this word by saying, "The cost of the project cannot balloon." Building on that statement, the team might identify that developing the training within budget is an issue and that developing within a certain cost is a business requirement. The agreed-on statement would then be written on a flip chart as a potential or initial business requirement.
>
> *Example 2:* The random word is *spacecraft.* The managing director might say, "It shouldn't take as long to build the training as it does to build a spacecraft." Building on this statement, the team might identify development duration as a factor and another business requirement that the training be developed within a certain amount of time. The agreed-on statement would then be written on a flip chart as another potential business requirement.

There are some things to watch out for when using random word. The team must be careful not to dismiss words quickly by deciding that a specific word is of no use and then selecting another instead. If the team does this, they are more likely than not trying to choose a word that neatly fits into the problem they are trying to solve, thus reducing the creative thinking. The team must also be careful not to create too many steps between the random word as a stimulus and the creation of a relevant idea.

Wishful Thinking Technique. The wishful thinking technique is useful for coming up with new ideas. Team members dream of their ideal situation or solution. In this case, team members call out the business requirement that they wish the training would meet. This technique can be effective because the team often comes up with something that is already known but is now presented in a more practical and realistic way. It can also be useful because when the team has something to aim for, it can be practical in considering how far it wants to go to meet that requirement. Some wishful questions that team members might ask themselves while generating solutions might be:

- What would my perfect solution be?
- What effect would my ideal solution have?
- What if money (or morals or laws) did not matter at all?
- What would I do if I had unlimited power and resources?
- What would my ideal solution look like?

Once the team has identified their perfect solutions, they look at how realistic and how practical the solutions would be in practice.

Random Picture Technique. This method is similar to the random word technique. Instead of using a word as a stimulus, it uses a picture. Some people find it easier to use pictures rather than words, and others vice versa. The team leader should experiment to see which works better for the team. The first requirement for this technique is a random picture that is used as a prompt to come up with new ideas and solutions. The team can select pictures at random from a magazine, encyclopedia, or picture book.

Team members look at the picture, extract a concept or idea from it, and use the idea to stimulate a possible solution to the problem. They should try to see anything in the picture that reminds them of the problem and how it might be solved. What activities are going on? What situations are being faced? Why are the people doing what they are doing? What principles are being used?

With the picture in front of them, team members extract ideas from it or imagine a similar theme, person, or action happening within their own situation or from their perspective. Next they think of how they can use that new situation, object, or attitude in their own situation.

As was the case with the random word technique, the team must be careful in deciding that a specific picture is of no use and choosing another. They should also be careful of linking the picture with an idea that they already know about. Team members must train their minds not to do this. They must take the picture at face value and not use the technique to come up with an old idea to show that the old idea is good.

Affinity Diagram Technique. The affinity diagram, or KJ method (named after its author, Kawakita Jiro), has become one of the most widely used Six Sigma brainstorming, management, and planning tools. The affinity diagram was developed to discover meaningful groups of ideas within a raw list. In doing so, it is important to let the groupings emerge naturally rather than according to preordained categories.

Typically an affinity diagram is used to refine a brainstorm into something that makes sense and can be dealt with more easily. Some experts recommend using the affinity diagram when the facts or thoughts are uncertain and need to be organized, when preexisting ideas or paradigms need to be overcome, when ideas need to be clarified, and when unity within a team needs to be created.

Steps in Constructing an Affinity Diagram

1. State the issue or problem to be explored. Start with a clear statement of the problem or goal, and provide a time limit for the session; usually forty-five to sixty minutes is sufficient.
2. Brainstorm ideas for the issue or problem. Each participant should think of ideas and write them individually on index cards or sticky notes, or have a recorder write them on a flip chart.
3. Collect the cards or sticky notes, mix them up, and spread them out (or stick them) on a flat surface, such as a desk or wall. Index cards can be secured to a wall with a putty-type adhesive.
4. Arrange the cards or sticky notes into related groups. For approximately fifteen minutes, allow participants to pick out cards that list related ideas and set them aside until all cards are grouped.
5. Create a title or heading for each grouping that best describes the theme of each group of cards (Figure 6.4).

One great benefit of using the affinity diagram as a brainstorming tool is that it not only helps the team to get the issues on the table but also to categorize the issues.

FIGURE 6.4. AFFINITY DIAGRAM.

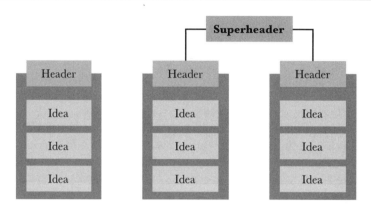

Rules for Brainstorming

Regardless of the tool used, there are certain rules that apply to any brainstorming session in order for it to be effective. This doesn't mean that the group can't have fun or be creative. It just means that there must be a code of conduct for people interacting with each other. When this code of conduct is breached, people stop being creative. The best way for there to be meaningful ground rules is for the team to create their own. This allows the team to take ownership of acceptable and unacceptable behaviors. There are, however, four key ground rules that are useful when conducting any brainstorming session:

- There are no dumb ideas. Period. It's a brainstorming session, not a serious matter that requires only serious solutions. This is one of the more fun tools of quality, so keep the entire team involved.
- Don't criticize any ideas. This isn't a debate, discussion, or forum for one person to display superiority over another.
- Build on ideas. Often an idea suggested by one person can trigger a bigger or better idea by another person. Or a variation of an idea on the board could be the next big idea. It is this building of ideas that leads to creative thinking and sparkling ideas.
- Reverse the thought of quality over quantity. Here the goal is quantity; the more creative the ideas are, the better. The facilitator can even make it a challenge to come up with as many ideas as possible and compare this team's performance to the previous brainstorming session he or she conducted.

Rules of Brainstorming

- There are no dumb ideas.
- Don't criticize other people's ideas.
- Build on other people's ideas.
- Reverse the thought of quality over quantity.

Refining the List of Business Requirements

At this point in the process, the team should have generated a list of business requirements. Since no judgment was made about the requirements, the list might be quite long, and the team may notice that some of the requirements appear to be very similar (and may well be the same solution stated differently). It is now time to filter the list in order to ensure that the final list contains the true requirements of the project stakeholders. One popular Six Sigma tool that can assist in this process is combine, delete, add, modify (CDAM).

Let's assume the team used affinity as the brainstorming tool. In this case, the team should now have a list of solutions written on index cards and placed on a flat surface grouped in a logical sequence. Team members now place the index cards that they believe are addressing the same requirement together and combine them into one requirement that is acceptable to the team. After that, the team discards any requirements that they now realize are not actual requirements. They then add to the list any new ideas that were missed, and finally, they modify any remaining requirements that needed updating.

Requirements-Driven Metrics

The current approach to gauging or measuring the success or effectiveness of training programs is largely driven by metrics or criteria decided on by the training department and based on a proprietary methodology that dictates to the business stakeholder what should be measured. Even when there is a cursory discussion between the business stakeholder and the training professional (in order for the training professional to get an understanding of the business driver behind the training), somehow the discussion about measuring the impact of the training comes back to Kirkpatrick's four levels of evaluation. This approach supposes that regardless of the industry, the corporate culture, or the reason

---

Continued

that the training is being requested, the effectiveness of the program can be measured only by monitoring four factors. The ambiguity on the part of 40 percent of the CEOs and one-third of the chief operating officers, along with the fact that only 7 percent of the CFOs participated in an Accenture high performance workforce study (2004) should indicate that this approach isn't working. These measures are not convincing the people who write the checks that training is having a positive impact on their bottom line.

The concept of requirements-driven metrics (RDM) reverses the current mind-set that is used for determining what metrics should be used to measure the impact that training has on an organization. With RDM rather than the training organization dictating to the business what should be measured and reported, the business requirements drive measurement decisions and thus the metrics that need to be captured. If, for example, the business was concerned only with course completion rate, that would be the only measurement that would be accounted for and reported about the training.

Measure Step 2: Prioritizing Business Requirements

Once the team has agreed on the list of business requirements, the next step in the process is to prioritize those requirements. All requirements are not created equal. If at some point later the team needs to negotiate on which requirements are crucial to meet, prioritizing now will make the decision easier. The Six Sigma tool set again contains several tools to assist the team with this endeavor: weighting, pairwise comparison, analytical hierarchy process, and silent multivoting (Figure 6.5).

FIGURE 6.5. TOOLS FOR PRIORITIZING BUSINESS REQUIREMENTS.

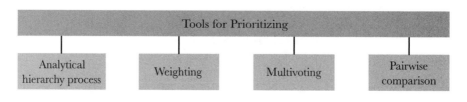

Weighting

With the weighting method, the list of requirements generated during the brainstorming session are listed on a flip chart. Using consensus, the team assigns a numerical value to each requirement, and the requirements are prioritized from the highest to the lowest number (Table 6.1). The benefit of using this technique is that it can be accomplished quickly with little or no training. The disadvantage is that it can be difficult for team members to distinguish a numerical difference between requirements that have similar importance. Disagreements on these issues can cause conflict between team members.

TABLE 6.1. WEIGHTING TABLE.

Requirement	Assigned Value
Requirement 1	1
Requirement 2	3
Requirement 3	5
Requirement 4	7
Requirement 5	3
Requirement 6	7
Requirement 7	1

Pairwise Comparison

Pairwise comparison is excellent at prioritizing requirements. With this method, each requirement is matched head-to-head with each of the other requirements. Requirements get 1 point for a one-on-one win and a ½ point for a tie. The requirements are then prioritized based on their scores.

Let's assume that four of the requirements identified by the business review team were speed to market, length of course, development cost, and the ability to reach many students quickly. To use pairwise comparison, the team leader would display all possible head-to-head match-ups. Consider Table 6.2, in which each requirement has a row and column assigned.

TABLE 6.2. PAIRWISE COMPARISON.

	Speed to Market	Length of Course	Development Cost	Reach
Speed to Market				
Length of Course				
Development Cost				
Reach				

The first step is to place asterisks in cells where the head-to-head match-ups would be the same requirement (Table 6.3).

TABLE 6.3. STEP 1 OF PAIRWISE COMPARISON.

	Speed to Market	Length of Course	Development Cost	Reach
Speed to Market	*			
Length of Course		*		
Development Cost			*	
Reach				*

The team would then select a head-to-head match-up, for example, between speed to market and length of course. The team leader might ask the team: "If we could have only speed to market or course length, which would it be?" The team would vote on the answer. If the length-of-course option were the winner, an arrow pointing to length of course would be put in the cell. If speed to market were the winning choice, an arrow pointing to that choice would be placed in the cell. If no consensus could be reached, a line would be placed in the cell (Table 6.4).

TABLE 6.4. STEP 2 OF PAIRWISE COMPARISON.

	Speed to Market	Length of Course	Development Cost	Reach
Speed to Market	*	↑		
Length of Course		*		
Development Cost			*	
Reach				*

Once the team has reached consensus on the first head-to-head match-up, the same question is asked about the next match-up. This questioning continues until each of the requirements has been compared to each other (see Table 6.5). Note that in Table 6.5 an asterisk is used whenever a requirement is compared to itself. For example, when "Development Time" in the left column intersects with "Development Time" on the top row an asterisk is placed in the intersecting cell. The arrows in the table are used to indicate which requirement wins the head-to-head match-up. For example, in the cell where "Cost" in the left column is compared with "Development Time," on the top row "Cost" is rated as more important, thus an arrow pointing to "Cost" is entered into the intersecting cell. In a case in which no decision can be made and both requirements are judged to be equal, a two-headed arrow is entered into the intersecting cell. For example, when "Reach" in the left column is compared with "Development Time" in the top row, the requirements are judged to be equal, thus a two-headed arrow is entered into the intersecting cells.

TABLE 6.5. COMPLETED PAIRWISE COMPARISON.

	Speed to Market	Length of Course	Development Cost	Reach
Speed to Market	*	↑	↑	↔
Length of Course	←	*	↑	↑
Development Cost	←	←	*	←
Reach	↔	←	↑	*

Each time a requirement wins a head-to-head match-up, it receives 1 point. The scores are calculated and the requirements ranked based on this comparison. Any ties in voting are broken by the results of the head-to-head comparison; for example, although course length and reach received the same score, reach would be ranked higher based on the head-to-head comparison (Table 6.6).

TABLE 6.6. REQUIREMENT TABULATION.

Development Time	Length of Course	Cost	Reach
0	2	6	2

The benefit of pairwise comparison is that it is accurate. The downside is that this method of prioritizing frequently leads to conflict.

Analytical Hierarchy Process

Analytical hierarchy process (AHP) is a combination of weighting and pairwise comparison. With this technique, each of the requirements established during brainstorming is compared against the others. In addition to identifying which requirement is more important, a numerical value is assigned to identify how much more important the choice is. A multiplier is then applied. This method causes each requirement to be assigned a numerical value automatically and objectively. This value is then used to rank the requirement (Table 6.7). The benefit of this technique is that it is extremely accurate. It also reduces contention among team members because of the objectivity. The downside of this technique is that it takes longer to complete than either weighting or pairwise comparison.

Silent Multivoting

The last technique that we look at is silent multivoting. This technique reduces contention between teammates because the vote is secret. At the beginning of this exercise, the number of requirements is counted, and each requirement is assigned a number. Each participant is given half the number of votes as there are requirements to cast. If a participant feels strongly, he or she may cast more than one vote for that requirement. Participants write down the numbers corresponding to the requirements that they would like to vote for on pieces of paper. These

TABLE 6.7. ANALYTICAL HIERARCHY PROCESS MATRIX.

Number of Requirements	4
Ratings Multiplier	10
"Less Important Than" Symbol	*

☐ = Not for user data entry

		Costs	Speed to Market	Ability to Reach 3,000 Users	Easy on Eyes			Rating
1	Cost	1	*	*	*			0.5
2	Speed to Market	3	1	*	*			0.9
3	Ability to Reach 3,000 Users	9	7	1	5			6.1
4	Minimum Resources	5	7	*	1			2.6
5								
6								
7								
8								
9								
10								

Note: "Not for user data entry" assumes an electronic spreadsheet is being used to calculate the ratings.

slips of paper are put into a hat or a bowl, and the votes are tallied, with the results deciding the prioritization of the requirements. The benefit of silent multi-voting is that it is quick and reduces debate. The downside is that if the directions are not made clear, it can take longer to complete.

Pros and Cons of Various Tools

All of these tools have pros and cons, which are set out in Table 6.8. As you can clearly see in the table, while the analytical hierachy process (AHP) and pairwise comparison are both accurate, AHP takes longer to complete and pairwise comparison can lead to conflict between team members. The quickest approach (weighting) is less accurate and can cause the team difficulty in distinguishing between requirements with similar importance. Silent multivoting is quick and reduces debate among team members, but it also takes longer to complete. Therefore, the team leader must judge the personality of the team and choose the approach that best suits the situation.

TABLE 6.8. PROS AND CONS OF VARIOUS TOOLS.

Tool	Pros	Cons
Silent multivoting	Quick, reduces debate	Takes longer to complete
Analytical hierarchy process	Accurate	Takes longer to complete
Pairwise comparison	Accurate	May lead to conflict between team members
Weighting	Quick	Hard to distinguish between requirements with similar importance

Measure Step 3: Translating Business Requirements into Measurable Targets

We now know what the business requirements are and their order of importance. The next step in the measure phase is to translate those requirements into targets that can be measured. This is a crucial component of the DMADDI process. If the business requirements are not quantified now, there is no way that at the end of the project, anyone will be able to objectively determine if the project has actually met its goals. This section looks at why it is necessary to convert business requirements into measurable targets. It also examines some tools for converting business requirements and explains how to convert business requirements into measurable targets.

It's All in the Translation

A father is running late for an appointment. His wife is supposed to be home to watch their infant, but she is caught in traffic and won't be home for another hour. The father looks at his watch. If he can leave in the next fifteen minutes, he can still make the meeting. Desperate, he picks up the telephone and calls his teenage son who is next door at his friend's house. "Noah, I need you to come home as soon as possible. I need you to watch your brother so that I can make my meeting." Forty minutes later, the son ambles into the house. The father, who has missed his meeting, is visibly upset. He looks at his son and says, "I thought I told you to come home as soon as possible." The son, clearly unaware of why his father is upset, replies, "I did."

The mistake that the father made is that he did not give a clear and precise target for his son to meet. His instruction or requirement ("as soon as possible") was interpreted one way by him and in another way by his son. The same situation occurs in the training world when a requirement is stated in a manner that leaves room for interpretation. "The training should be engaging" or "I need it fast" are requirements that might be interpreted differently by different stakeholders. Ensuring that business requirements are written in a manner that leaves no room for interpretation prevents the training manager from being left at home holding the baby and missing the meeting.

Tools for Converting Business Requirements

The Six Sigma tool chest contains several options that are useful in converting or translating business requirements into measurable targets (Figure 6.6). The two

FIGURE 6.6. TOOLS FOR CONVERTING BUSINESS REQUIREMENTS.

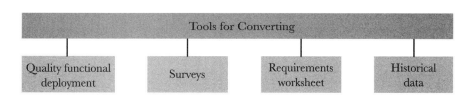

most popular are the requirements worksheet and quality functional deployment (QFD).

Requirements Statement Worksheet. The requirements statement worksheet is used to identify what is important to stakeholders. The team members list the comments that they have been receiving from stakeholders, convert the comments into issues, and convert the issues into measurable requirements (Table 6.9). For example, a stakeholder says, "Every time my employees go to one of your classes, I lose them for two days." This comment might be translated into to an issue titled "course length." After interviewing or having discussions with process partners, the team gets agreement that they are willing to lose employees for no longer than one day. The business requirement thus becomes that the "course shall be no longer than one day."

TABLE 6.9. REQUIREMENTS STATEMENT WORKSHEET.

Business Comment	Image or Issue	Requirement
1. "Every time my employees go to one of your classes, I lose them for two days."	Course length	Course will be no longer than one day.
2. "I only have $20,000 in my training budget."	Cost	Program will be developed for $10,000 or less.
3. "What's this training going to do for me anyway?"	Quantifiable measures	All students must demonstrate mastery (90 percent or better) in a simulation of the system's five functions.

Quality Functional Deployment. Quality functional deployment (QFD) is a demanding but highly effective tool that can be used across virtually every phase of DMADDI. It is an iterative process for continually refining customer requirements. With this tool, business and customer input is translated into basic design elements that are then translated into product specifications. The product specifications are translated into design features, which are translated into performance specs. In the measure phase, this tool is used as follows:

1. The business or customer requirements are listed in column 1.
2. Column 2 contains the importance as determined during prioritization.

3. For each business or customer requirement listed, the team assigns a measurable design requirement. The design requirements are in columns that intersect with their corresponding customer requirement.

In Table 6.10, for example, customer requirement 2 is cost, and the corresponding design requirement is developed for $10,000. This target leaves no room for ambiguity. It is a measurable business requirement. If the solution costs more than $10,000, the business target has not been met.

TABLE 6.10. QUALITY FUNCTIONAL DEPLOYMENT.

Customer requirements/ Design requirements	Importance	Length of program no longer than one day	Program shall cost no more than $10,000	Program must reach 3,000 students in one month	Development must be complete within three months	Program must contain facility for measurement
Length	2	X				
Cost	6		X			
Reach	0			X		
Time	2				X	
Measurement	1					X

A Note About Business Requirements

Requirements tend to come in the form of subjective statements about what a stakeholder is seeking from a product. Team members might think they understand the meaning of a particular statement but in fact tend to interpret statements in different ways. This difference of interpretation often does not become evident until the team attempts to define ways to satisfy the requirements. The process of translating requirements into design measures is a way to force the team to define, using measurable and actionable statements, exactly what each requirement means in the language of the organization. For example, a customer requirement for an e-learning program might be, "Is easy to access." Instructional designers would be left to their own interpretation as to whether the training would really satisfy their customers. Through the QFD process, a team might define the following measures for "is easy to access":

- User rating of screen layout concepts
- Number of user operations required to perform the desired functions
- Number of clicks required to perform the desired functions

Pros and Cons of Various Tools

The two tools examined here have their pros and cons, which are set out in Table 6.11. As the table shows, the requirements statement worksheet is the quickest approach, however, one of its shortcomings is that it might cause the team to miss important targets. Quality functional deployment, on the other hand, is a flexible tool that can be used across various phases in DMADDI, however it does not categorize and it can take a long time to complete. As was the case with the tools for prioritizing requirements, the team leader must choose the right tool for the team.

TABLE 6.11. PROS AND CONS OF VARIOUS TOOLS TRANSLATING REQUIREMENTS.

Tool	Pros	Cons
Requirements statement worksheet	Quick	Can miss important targets
Quality functional deployment	Multifunctional	Can take a long time to complete; does not categorize

Measure Step 4: Complete the Measure Tollgate

With the business requirements identified, prioritized, and quantified, the team is ready to validate that it has accomplished everything required in the measure phase and present the findings to the project champion. As was the case in the define phase, the team should complete a measure checklist to validate and get formal agreement from the team that all measure requirements have been met.

At the end of the measure phase, the following questions must be answered:

- Have the business requirements been identified?
- Have the business requirements been prioritized?
- Has the team identified measurable targets for each business requirement?
- Has the team updated the storyboard?

Measure Step 5: Transfer Requirements to the Development Team

Now that a charter has been established and the business requirements for the project have been identified, the work of creating the training solution is about to begin, and the role of the business review team now changes to one of oversight. The team will now pass all of its findings, including the project charter and business targets, to the development team so that it can begin creating a learning solution that meets the business requirements. The business review team will now have the responsibility of assessing the progress of the development team by validating at the end of each of the rest of the phases that the project is on target to meet business requirements. The bridge between the two teams is the Black Belt, who will also serve as the project lead on the development team. Prior to completing the measure phase, the team should complete the DMADDI Measure Checklist (see Exhibit 6.1) to insure that they have achieved all of the goals of the phase.

EXHIBIT 6.1. DMADDI MEASURE CHECKLIST.

Instructions: Respond appropriately to the following questions.

1. Has a list of business requirements for the project been agreed to?	
2. Have the business requirements been prioritized?	
3. Have all of the business requirements been assigned a measurable target?	
4. Has the team updated the storyboard?	
Comments:	
Team Member Signatures:	

DMADDI Tools for Measure

Random Word

Purpose: To generate new ideas

When to Use

- Whenever there is a need to complete a brainstorming activity where new ideas or solutions need to be generated

Steps to Follow

1. Choose a word from a random word generator such as a dictionary or book.
2. Extract its underlying principles, and apply them to the problem.
3. Establish a bridging idea, which is an idea based on the stimulus.
4. Generate ideas.
5. List the ideas generated on a flip chart.

Wishful Thinking

Purpose: To generate solutions

When to Use

- Anytime there is a requirement to generate creative solutions to obstacles facing a team

Steps to Follow

1. Have team members dream of their ideal situation or solution.
2. Team members call out the requirement they wish the training would address
3. Evaluate how realistic the solution would be in practice.

Weighting

Purpose: To prioritize solutions

When to Use

- When a list of solutions has been generated and there is a need to prioritize those solutions

Steps to Follow

1. List the requirements generated during the brainstorming session on a flip chart.
2. Using consensus, assign a numerical value to each idea.
3. Prioritize the ideas from the highest to the lowest number.

Pairwise Comparison

Purpose: To prioritize solutions or requirements

When to Use

- When there is a need to prioritize a list of solutions or ideas

Steps to Follow

1. Compare each requirement against all other requirements.
2. Rank the requirements based on this comparison.

Analytical Hierarchy Process

Purpose: To prioritize a list of requirements or solutions

When to Use

- Whenever there is a need to prioritize a list of solutions or ideas

Steps to Follow

1. Compare each of the ideas established during brainstorming against the others.
2. Assign a numerical value to each idea to identify how much more important the choice is. Apply a multiplier.
3. Use the numerical value to rank the idea, solution, or requirement.

TABLE 6.12. ANALYTICAL HIERARCHY PROCESS MATRIX.

Number of Requirements	4
Ratings Multiplier	10
"Less Important Than" Symbol	*

☐ = Not for user data entry

		Costs	Speed to Market	Ability to Reach 3,000 Users	Easy on Eyes			Rating
1	Cost	1	*	*	*			0.5
2	Speed to Market	3	1	*	*			0.9
3	Ability to Reach 3,000 Users	9	7	1	5			6.1
4	Minimum Resources	5	7	*	1			2.6
5								
6								
7								
8								
9								
10								

Note: "Not for user data entry" assumes an electronic spreadsheet is being used to calculate the ratings.

Quality Functional Deployment

TABLE 6.13. QUALITY FUNCTIONAL DEPLOYMENT MATRIX.

Customer Requirements / Design Requirements	Important	Web-Based Deployment	Project Team of Five	Deployed in Sixty Days	Developed for $20,000
Ability to Reach 3,000 Users					
Minimum Resources					
Speed to Market					
Cost					
Metric		K	P	D	$
USL		4K	5	60	20K
Target		3K	5	60	20K
LSL		3K	3	45	15K

Purpose: To convert requirements into measurable targets

When to Use

- At any time when there is a need to refine or convert the voice of the customer into measurable targets

Steps to Follow

1. List the business or customer requirements in column 1.
2. Enter the importance (as was determined during prioritization) in column 2.
3. For each business or customer requirement listed, assign a measurable design requirement.

Requirements Statement Worksheet

TABLE 6.14. REQUIREMENTS STATEMENT WORKSHEET.

Business Comment	Image or Issue	Requirement

Purpose: To convert business requirements into measurable targets

When to Use

- At any point in the project when there is a need to refine or convert the voice of the business into measurable targets

Steps to Follow

1. List all business comments in column 1.
2. Categorize each of the requirements identified.
3. Assign a measurable target to each requirement.

Summary

This chapter focused on the second phase of the DMADDI methodology: measure. This is where the business requirements of a project are fleshed out and the voices of the customer and business are identified, prioritized, and quantified. This chapter addressed identifying business requirements, prioritizing business requirements, and then translating those business requirements into measurable targets. It explained brainstorming and prioritization tools that help team members flesh out a project's business requirements.

The next chapter discusses the phase that answers the question, "What needs to be learned?" The analyze phase of DMADDI is where the work to construct the learning solution begins. The role of the business review team changes to one of oversight, and the focus shifts to the development team. The next chapter therefore focuses on the work done by the development team and the Six Sigma tools that will assist them in the effort.

CHAPTER SEVEN

ANALYZE

What Needs to Be Learned?

Analyze is the phase of **DMADDI** where the learning requirements for the project are identified: it asks, "What needs to be learned"? (Figure 7.1). It is also where the work to construct the learning solution begins. At this point in the process, the role of the business review team changes from that of a working group to one of an oversight committee, and the focus of the project shifts to the design team, which will put together the learning solution.

This chapter focuses on the work that needs to be accomplished by that cross-functional group. It also highlights the Six Sigma tools that will assist the team in their efforts. This chapter explains what happens in the analyze phase of DMADDI. It sets out techniques for choosing design team members, gaining a deeper understanding of the process, and focusing on Six Sigma tools for identifying, prioritizing, and validating what needs to be learned.

DMADDI Road Map

In order to answer the question, "What needs to be learned?" a design team is formed. This team engages in activities that identify exactly what needs to be learned. After that, the team validates and prioritizes the learning requirements. Finally a tollgate is undertaken to ensure that everything identified in the analyze phase agrees with the outputs from the previous phases.

FIGURE 7.1. DMADDI ROAD MAP FOR ANALYZE.

Define	What are the business requirements?
Measure	What targets do we need to meet?
Analyze	What needs to be learned?
Design	How should we teach it?
Develop	Does our prototype match our design?
Implement	Did the implementation meet business and instructional requirements?

This approach to designing training programs might be compared to a software development project where a number of teams are formed or exist to support the overall project. The team responsible for the decision to create the new software product is different from the team responsible for developing the product. And that team has different responsibilities than does the team responsible for marketing the product. Each team has its individual objective and charter even though all are individually contributing to the overall strategic goal.

The analyze phase of DMADDI is different from the analysis phase in ISD in a few ways. In DMADDI, the business decisions and business requirements for the training project are made before the learning analysis takes place. Business professionals who are trained, and whose job it is to run businesses, perform the business analysis. This model frees the instructional designer to practice the essential competencies of instructional design and for the design team to focus solely on learning requirements, what needs to be learned, and the best way to teach it.

This phase is supported by an overall project structure that is designed to ensure project success. There is no such project structure associated with ISD.

As we discussed in Chapter Four, in the DMADDI project structure (Figure 7.2), the project champion requests the training and is responsible for setting the initial vision. The business review team sets the business requirements, determines the business targets and thus what constitutes return on investment, and oversees the process to ensure that any decisions made will not compromise the program's ability to meet business requirements. The design team identifies the learning requirements and is responsible for ensuring that those targets are met. The project leader is the glue that ties all of the stakeholders and processes together.

FIGURE 7.2. DMADDI PROJECT ORGANIZATION.

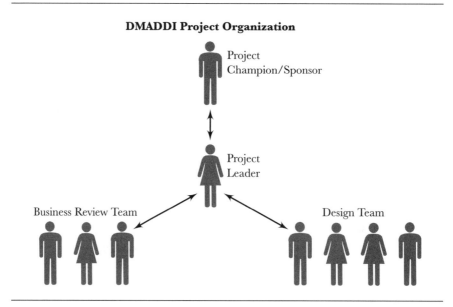

The project leader is responsible for assembling the design team. Once the team is assembled, its roles and responsibilities must be established and a team charter created. The leader also has to guide the team in identifying, validating, and prioritizing learning objectives; ensuring that they are quantified; and ensuring that an analysis tollgate is completed (Figure 7.3).

FIGURE 7.3. DMADDI ANALYZE ACTIVITIES.

Objective	Activities	Tools	Deliverables
To determine what needs to be learned	Needs assessment Problem identification Task analysis Population analysis	Task analysis Population analysis Surveys Fishbone diagrams Affinity diagrams	Learner profile Task analysis Description of constraints Quantifiable learning requirements Analyze tollgate

Analyze Step 1: Assembling a Design Team

In DMADDI, the first step in the analyze phase is to identify and put together a design team. The potential team members may have already been identified during the define phase when a stakeholder analysis was done. There are pros and cons of identifying design team members during the define phase. One benefit of identifying design team members during the stakeholder analysis that occurs during the define phase is that it gives the project leader the ability and opportunity to give early notice to these people. This early notice allows them to free their schedules for the meetings that they will need to attend later. One con, however, is that during the define phase, the business review team members may change their minds on who the correct person is based on what is discovered at that point. Informing someone that he or she may be part of the project and then later reversing that may have negative repercussions. It is therefore recommended that design team members not be identified until the analyze phase.

Design Team

If the design team members were not identified during the define phase, the project leader can now take advantage of the stakeholder analysis to identify the team members. The same process that was followed while completing the form during the define phase should be adhered to in the analyze phase, with one exception: the criterion for selecting design team members is different. Design team members should be stakeholders who have helpful expertise and are not part of the business review team. Since the steps to completing a stakeholder analysis were covered in Chapter Five, I will not repeat it here. Exhibit 7.1 shows what a completed stakeholder analysis done during the analyze phase might look like.

As Exhibit 7.1 shows, many of those who will be members of the design team are to report directly to members of the business review team. This relationship makes it easier to gain cooperation from design team members and opens the lines of communication across the project. However, the team is not considered assembled until each of the team members has agreed to his or her role and responsibility on the project. As was the case with the business review team, this is accomplished with a team charter.

Design Charter

Putting together a charter for design team members doesn't take as much work as putting together the DMADDI charter. Much of the information required for the charter for the design team is derived from the DMADDI project charter. While it may seem like extra work, creating this charter is nevertheless an important task. Although the design and the business review team are both associated with the overall project, they are separate teams with different roles and responsibilities. Everyone involved with the project must be clear about the charter of their team and clear about their roles as individuals.

Analyze Step 2: Identifying What Needs to Be Learned

Once the design team has agreed on the team charter, they can get to work determining what the students who will be taking the training program need to learn. This task can be accomplished by engaging in a variety of activities that should be familiar to any instructional designer:

- Training needs assessment: Reviewing and surveying the requests of significant stakeholders in order to determine the nature and symptoms of a performance problem and identifying the underlying causes
- Job-task analysis: Clearly delineating the major functions, roles, tasks, and outcomes of a targeted job; deducing from the job-task analysis the scope of training, sequencing of instruction, prerequisites, equipment, and tools used and the acceptable standards of job performance

EXHIBIT 7.1. DMADDI STAKEHOLDER ANALYSIS FORM.

Stakeholder	Relationship to Project					Involvement Strategy					
	Is Affected by Outcome	Can Influence Outcome	Has Helpful Expertise	Provides Resources	Has Decision Authority	Meet with Regularly	Invite to Meetings	Speak with Informally	Copy on Meeting Minutes	Business Review Team Member	Development Team Member
Managing director	X	X		X	X				X	X	
Accounting manager	X	X	X	X	X	X		X	X	X	
Product manager			X	X					X		X
Product developer			X						X		
Accountants	X		X			X		X	X	X	
Instructional designer		X	X			X		X	X		X
Training manager	X	X	X	X	X				X	X	
SME accountant	X	X	X					X	X		X

- Learner analysis: Specifying the target audience for training and analyzing its members' knowledge, skills, attitudes, and competencies to determine what they already know and what they need to learn to become fully proficient
- Context analysis: Documenting the characteristics of the learning environment

There are several tools that the traditional ISD approach to training development employs in order to accomplish these activities. Here we focus on some of the Six Sigma tools that are helpful with this endeavor.

When to Use Six Sigma Tools

Six Sigma tools for identifying learning requirements are especially useful when there are several layers of individuals who must review, approve, or simply look at the topics that will be covered in the course. If there is ambiguity about who the approvers are or if several layers of approval are required, Six Sigma tools can reduce or even eliminate the time-consuming back-and-forth review cycles that often take place in order to get course content approved. To better illustrate the point, let's take a look at what typically occurs when the most popular ISD approaches are used to get course objectives approved.

The instructional designer interviews an SME to identify the topics that must be covered in the course and then tries to turn these topics into learning objectives. Once the objectives have been written, they are sent to the SME for his or her review and approval. At that point, things get muddy. The SME may want to show the objectives to others in his or her area to make sure that nothing was missed. The objectives might then go from person to person over a period of days, weeks, or even months, with content being added, changed, and deleted at each step.

At some point, the SME gets the comments back and forwards them to the instructional designer, who must then rewrite the content so that the topics resemble learning objectives. Then the designer might send the objectives back to the SME for final approval. But the SME now remembers two or three items that he or she forgot to mention earlier and also removes two or three of the items that were added during the previous review. The content is again sent to the instructional designer, who again cleans up the objectives and again sends the material to the SME. This time the SME wants his or her boss to take a look at the topics. The boss, of course, has a different take on the course and makes large changes that are again sent to the instructional designer to clean up.

Frustrated, the instructional designer attempts to put an end to the review and approval process. She sends an e-mail to the SME: "Once I make these changes, can I consider the objectives approved?" The SME replies, "Yes." Relieved, the instructional designer begins to clean up the objectives. But just as she is ready to send out the final approved objectives, she receives a call from the SME: "My boss wants product and operations to look at the objective before we move on."

This is probably familiar to any instructional designer who has spent any amount of time creating courses in an organization of any size. The next section highlights some Six Sigma tools that can reduce the pain associated with this type of interaction.

Useful Six Sigma Tools

Six Sigma has two very useful tools that if applied to identifying learning objectives can eliminate this type of back-and-forth endless review of the required topics. One of these tools is the affinity diagram, which was covered in Chapter Six. The other is referred to as either deployment flowchart or deployment mapping. Let's look at how each of these tools might be applied to identifying learning requirements and how both can eliminate the review cycles.

Affinity Diagrams. We initially learned about affinity in Chapter Five. In Chapter Six, affinity diagrams were used in order to identify business requirements. Using affinity diagrams to determine learning requirements is similar. The first step is to get all the right people in one room at the same time. The SME must be there. If we continue to use the accounting scenario from earlier in the book, the product developer should be there. Although they may not be design team members, if the other accountants are going to have input, then they should be in the room. Having everyone who has input into the learning topics together at the same time eliminates content being passed from person to person without the context or the rationale that went into determining that the topic should be covered.

The team leader can either have all the participants write on index cards every topic that they think needs to be covered, or he or she can have the participants call out the topics that they think must be covered and have a volunteer write these topics on stickies and place them on a flat surface. There are a few psychological benefits of using stickies or index cards to record information. One is that if it is decided that a topic was listed in error, the sticky or index card can simply be removed from the board. If the team changes its mind about the topic, it is easy to replace the card or sticky. Erasing someone's comments from a whiteboard has a different psychological effect. Once the participants have exhausted their input to the idea generation process, the team leader can lead the team in performing CDAM to filter the list. Then the team can organize the remaining topics into what the group thinks are logical groupings. Once they have agreed on the list and their groupings, the only remaining task is for the instructional designer to reword the topics so that they are legitimate learning objectives.

This method allows everyone who needs to participate in determining the learning topics to participate in determining the course content. And it does it in a way that eliminates the ongoing review and approval process that plagues ISD.

Deployment Flowchart. A deployment flowchart is a detailed flowchart of a process that shows not only what activities take place in a process, but also who is responsible for the activity. This tool is especially useful when the training will cover a process and the process requires frequent handoffs or when there are many people involved in the process.

As is the case with affinity diagrams, it is important to get everyone who will have input to the learning topics in the same room at the same time. There must be representation of all the people associated with the process. We'll use the new accounting program described earlier as an example.

We'll assume that the participants in the room are the accountant SME, the product developer, another accountant, the team leader, and the instructional designer. Once the group is assembled, the team leader might post flip chart paper around the walls of the room, number each chart, and then ask, "Okay, team, with this new program, what are the major tasks that we can accomplish?" One of the accountants might call out "reconciling accounts receivable." "Great," replies the leader. "Let's start with that process." At the top of the first chart, the leader writes RECONCILING ACCOUNTS RECEIVABLE and then asks, "Who are the people involved with this process?" As the team members call out the names or titles of the people involved, the instructional designer writes the names from top to bottom on page 1 of the flip chart.

Once the players have been identified, the leader might ask, "What is the first step in the process?" The product developer answers, "The system sends a notification." The project leader would then probe, "Who gets the notification?" The accountant answers, "I do." At that point, the instructional designer places a circle at the same level as the accountant. The leader then asks, "What happens next?" The accountant replies, "I log on to the new system." The instructional designer places a box at the same level as the accountant but to the right of the circle and in the box writes LOG INTO SYSTEM.

The leader continues the questioning: "What happens next?" The accountant responds, "I check the reason codes." Again, at the same level as the accountant and to the right of the first box, the instructional designer creates another box and in it writes CHECK REASON CODES. The leader asks, "Then what?" "Well, it depends," responds the accountant. "If the reason code is below 25, I send it to my supervisor. If it is above 100, I route it to finance." Next to the box at the same level as the accountant, the instructional designer creates a diamond and in it writes BELOW 25?.

The questioning continues: "If the reason code is below 25 and is routed to your supervisor, what happens once he gets the notification?" The answer is, "He researches the history of the transaction." The instructional designer then draws a box to the right of the diamond, but this time at the level of the accounting manager and in the box writes RESEARCH TRANSACTION HISTORY. Figure 7.4 is an example of what a cross-functional deployment flowchart might look like.

FIGURE 7.4. SAMPLE DEPLOYMENT MAP
FOR RECONCILING ACCOUNTS RECEIVABLE.

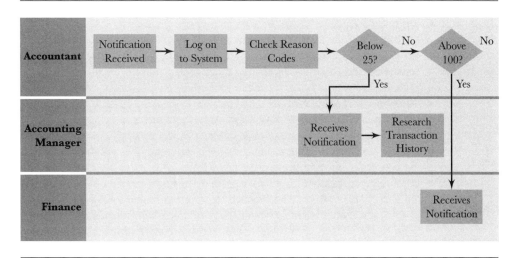

Tip: Creating a Process Flow Diagram

It is critical when creating a process flow diagram to include the small steps in the process flow. Make the process flow on a micro basis rather than a macro basis.

The questioning and flowcharting continue until the entire process is represented in graphical form. The team then engages in discussion to validate that what appeared on the flip charts represents what occurs in the process. The boxes represent the major tasks. Further questioning would uncover the subtasks: "What must you do in order to check reason codes?" "What are the steps involved with researching transaction history?" After all of the subtasks have been identified, the designer can convert them into objectives.

While grueling as a process, deployment flowcharting gets everyone who might have input into course objectives working together. As was the case with the affinity diagram, this technique eliminates the ongoing review and approval process associated with ISD. The process also creates a natural grouping or organization for the course.

Key Points for Assembling a Deployment Flowchart

- A process flow diagram is a detailed picture of a process. It represents the logical flow of activities from the beginning of the process to the end. For example, the receipt of a handwritten memo may be the beginning of the typing process and an error-free typed memo may be the end of the process.
- When drawing a process flow diagram, consider what the starting and ending points are. Process flow diagrams help a team or individual gain an understanding of the steps in a process.
- Process flow diagrams are useful as training tools and as a method of gaining consensus on what the process actually is.
- When you create a process flow diagram with your team on a piece of flip chart paper with markers, you'll often get four or five steps into the process and then a team member will remember a loop that should have been added. Inserting the step is hard, and sometimes impossible, to do; often you feel you have to start over with a clean piece of paper. An excellent way around this problem is to create the process flow diagram using sticky notes.

Analyze Step 3: Validating and Prioritizing What Needs to Be Learned

Now that the objectives have been identified, the team should review what was identified in order to validate that they got it right; then they should prioritize the objectives. All objectives are not created equal, and if during the design phase certain learning topics must be omitted, prioritizing now will make the decision easier later. This step is readily accomplished by using any one of the tools already discussed: multivoting, weighting, or analytical hierarchy process. Each of these tools is equally effective at prioritizing and validating learning topics. If the team used deployment flowcharting to identify the learning requirements, however, silent multivoting might be the best choice for prioritizing the learning requirements. Using two tools back to back that cause contention might not be a good idea.

Regardless of the tool used to prioritize the objectives, contention between members can be reduced if the findings are presented in a nonthreatening manner. One Six Sigma tool that is useful in presenting data or information in a way that is nonintrusive yet will allow the team to quickly identify which objectives are the most important (at least based on what the team thinks) is the Pareto diagram.

The Pareto diagram is a special type of bar chart used to determine which problem to work on first to improve a process. It can also be used to identify which issue holds the highest priority. The diagram was developed by Italian economist Vilfredo Pareto in the late 1800s and is based on what is now called the Pareto principle. Pareto found that 80 percent of Italy's wealth was held by only 20 percent of the people. This 80/20 rule is generally true for many things. The Pareto diagram reduces the contention among team members because it takes the subjectivity out of interpreting data by presenting the results in a graphical format.

This powerful yet simple tool permits groups to reach consensus on what the major problem is. Since the diagram is based on data, it is difficult to argue over which problems (or, in this case, which learning objectives) are most important. If the team used silent voting as a method to determine which objectives were the most important, presenting a picture of the results removes any need for interpretation and allows team members to quickly grasp the results.

Constructing a Pareto diagram is fairly simple and straightforward. The instructions that follow describe how to construct the diagram manually, although there are many software programs that automate the production of Pareto diagrams based on data input. The instructions here assume that the team used multivoting as a selection method:

1. Determine the objectives to be identified on the diagram.
2. Total the frequency of occurrence for each objective.
3. Draw the x- and y-axes, putting the proper units on the y-axis.
4. Under the x-axis, write in the most important problem (largest frequency) first, then the next most important, and so on.
5. Draw in the bars. The height of the bar will correspond to the frequency of occurrence for each objective on the x-axis.
6. Calculate the cumulative percentages.
7. Plot the cumulative percentage line.
8. Title the graph, and include any other important information.

Let's take a look at how our design team might implement the Pareto diagram:

The team leader would like to present the results of the silent voting exercise. He wants the team to agree on which objectives are the most important:

1. Determine the objectives to be used on the diagram. The objectives were determined in the first step of the analyze phase. The team either brainstormed or used deployment flowcharting to list the objectives:

- Reconciling accounts receivable
- Interpret system notification
- Log on to system
- Interpret reason codes
- Notify appropriate supervisor
- Input correct data

2. Total the frequency of votes for each objective (Table 7.1).

TABLE 7.1. FREQUENCY TABLE.

Objective	Votes
Reconcile accounts receivable	3
Interpret system notification	8
Log on to system	1
Interpret reason codes	6
Notify appropriate supervisor	4
Input correct data	2

3. Draw the x- and y-axes, putting the proper units on the y-axis. Since the Pareto diagram will include the cumulative line, the maximum value on the y-axis should be at least equal to the total number of problems (reasons). The total number is eight. There are six different reasons. Therefore, the x-axis is divided into six equal segments (Figure 7.5).

4. Draw in the bars. The height of the bar will correspond to the frequency of occurrence for each problem on the x-axis. If possible, it is a good idea to write in the actual frequency on the top of each bar (Figure 7.6).

5. Calculate the cumulative percentage. The cumulative percentage is calculated as shown in Table 7.2. In this table, the data are given in descending order based on frequency of occurrence.

FIGURE 7.5. PARETO SEGMENTED CHART OF OBJECTIVES.

FIGURE 7.6. PARETO CHART OF OBJECTIVES
WITH FREQUENCY OF OCCURRENCE.

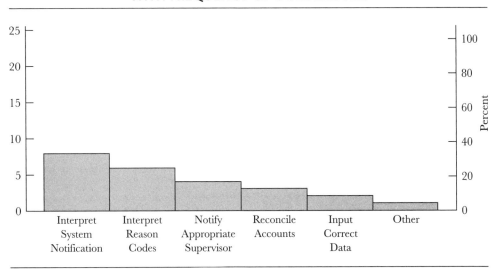

TABLE 7.2. CUMULATIVE PERCENTAGES.

	Interpret System Notification	Interpret Reason Codes	Notify Appropriate Supervisor	Reconcile Accounts	Input Correct Data	Other
Count	8	6	4	3	2	1
Percentage	33.3	25.0	16.7	12.5	8.3	4.2
Cumulative percentage	33.3	58.3	75.0	87.5	95.8	100.00

6. Plot the cumulative percentage (Figure 7.7). The 100 percent mark on the cumulative percentage axis corresponds to the total number of occurrences on the frequency axis.

FIGURE 7.7. FINAL PARETO CHART OF OBJECTIVES.

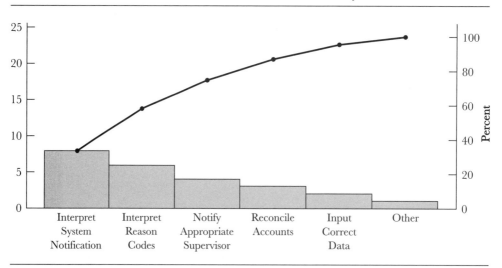

7. Title the graph, and include any other important information.

Once the team has reached agreement on the prioritization of the course objectives, it is ready to move on to the last step of the analyze phase: the analyze tollgate.

Analyze Step 4: Complete the Analyze Tollgate

The analyze tollgate is the first tollgate that the members of the design team will be involved with. At this meeting, the members of the design team will be reporting their findings to the business review team and the project sponsor. This formal presentation should be facilitated by the project leader, but each member of the design team should have a role. Prior to the tollgate, the team should be diligent in completing the analyze checklist (Exhibit 7.2) and preparing and practicing for the presentation. The storyboard should be updated, and team members should spend time validating among themselves how their findings will affect the business requirements of the project.

EXHIBIT 7.2. DMADDI ANALYZE CHECKLIST.

Instructions: Respond appropriately to the following questions.

1. Have members of the development team been identified?	
2. Has each member of the design team committed to the project?	
3. Has the team charter been approved by all team members?	
4. Has the team agreed to the learning requirements?	
5. Have the learning requirements been prioritized?	
6. Have the learning requirements been quantified?	
Comments:	
Team Member Signatures:	

As was the case with the business review team, having the entire design team involved has some benefits: there is an opportunity for team building, working together helps to break down cross-functional silos, and all team members get exposure to a more senior level of management.

At the end of the analyze phase, the following questions must be answered:

- Have members of the design team been identified?
- Has each member of the design team committed to the project?
- Has the team agreed to the course objectives?
- Has the team prioritized the course objectives?
- Is the project still on target to meet business requirements?

DMADDI Tools for Analyze

Deployment Flowchart

FIGURE 7.8. SAMPLE DEPLOYMENT MAP FOR RECONCILING ACCOUNTS RECEIVABLE.

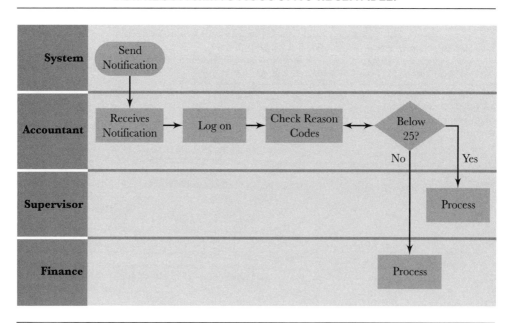

Purpose: To identify business review team members

When to Use

- To identify all of the steps that take place in a process

Steps to Follow

1. Brainstorm and list potential project stakeholders.
2. Ask the team to identify the first step in the process.

Affinity

Purpose: To determine learning requirements

When to Use

- When there is a need to generate ideas or requirements from a team

Steps to Follow

1. Have the participants call out the topics that they think must be covered.
2. Have a volunteer write these topics on stickies, and place them on a flat surface.
3. Perform CDAM (described in Chapter Five) to filter the list.
4. Organize the remaining topics into what the group thinks are logical groupings.
5. Reword the topics so that they are legitimate learning objectives.

Pareto Diagrams

Purpose: To identify which problem to work on first or to identify which issue holds the highest priority

When to Use

- When there is a need to determine which problem to work on first

Steps to Follow

1. Determine the objectives to be used on the diagram.
2. Total the frequency of occurrences for each objective.
3. Draw the x- and y-axes, putting the proper units on the y-axis.
4. Under the x-axis, write in the most important problem (largest frequency) first, then the next most important, and so on.
5. Draw in the bars. The height of the bar will correspond to the frequency of occurrence for each objective on the x-axis.

6. Calculate the cumulative percentages.
7. Plot the cumulative percentage line.
8. Title the graph, and include any other important information.

Summary

This chapter focused on the analyze phase, when the question, "What needs to be learned?" is answered. This phase is where the work to construct the learning solution begins and the role of the business review team changes from a working group to one of oversight. The focus of the project shifts to the design team. Therefore, the chapter addressed the work done by this team and introduced the Six Sigma tools that assist in that effort. The chapter also identified exactly what happens in the analyze phase, looked at techniques for choosing design team members, and discussed some of the Six Sigma tools that are useful for identifying and validating what needs to be learned.

CHAPTER EIGHT

DESIGN

How Should We Teach It?

This chapter concentrates on the design phase of DMADDI, when the question, "How do we teach it?" is answered. The work and focus of this phase of DMADDI remain with the design team. The business review team continues in its role as the oversight committee, ensuring that the work that occurs during design keeps the project on track to meet the project's business requirements. As was the case with the analyze phase of DMADDI, there is no shortage of books or articles on how to use the various training tools in order to identify how to teach certain topics. This chapter therefore continues to focus on Six Sigma tools that can be used to supplement this process.

DMADDI Road Map

Design is the phase of any training development project that instructional designers enjoy the most. In fact, this is when the majority of the essential competencies for instructional designers are put to use. The focal point of this chapter is on using Six Sigma tools in order to help the design team answer the question, "How should we teach it?" (Figure 8.1).

FIGURE 8.1. DMADDI ROAD MAP FOR DESIGN.

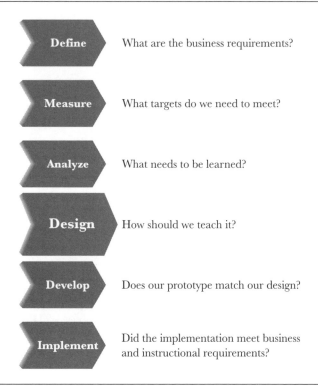

Define   What are the business requirements?

Measure   What targets do we need to meet?

Analyze   What needs to be learned?

Design   How should we teach it?

Develop   Does our prototype match our design?

Implement   Did the implementation meet business
              and instructional requirements?

Design in ISD

Design is considered the blueprinting stage when the instructional designer determines what needs to be learned. He or she accomplishes this by identifying the specifications necessary to complete the project, writing the learning objectives, developing test items, constructing course content, planning or developing instructional strategies and methods, and identifying resources.

With ISD methodology, virtually all of the work that is accomplished now is done independently by the instructional designer. Both Daniel J. Ford, author of *Designing Training Programs* (1996), and Don Clarke, who hosts a Web site providing free training, instructional design, and performance resources, http://www.nwlink.com/~donclark/hrd/sat.html, concur with this assessment. Ford, for example, states that during design, the instructional designer creates the following parts of the instruction system:

- Learning objectives
- Course content
- Instructional strategies and methods
- Evaluation and design plan
- Resources requirements (for example, money, time, personnel, equipment)

This practice of the instructional designer's independently creating this material is largely responsible for much of the back-and-forth review and approval process that takes place when this methodology is used.

In practice, learning objectives, tasks, course sequence, content, and assessment questions must typically be approved by at least one, and most times several, of the project's process partners. Having the instructional designer complete these tasks in isolation causes a condition where his or her outputs are "thrown over the fence" to a reviewer or approver with no context and no background on the decision-making process that caused the designer to come up with the results. This practice is a recipe for rework and frustration.

Design in DMADDI

Design in DMADDI (Figure 8.2) is different from the same phase in ISD in several ways. Perhaps the most glaring difference is the team concept. Almost all of the work done on any Six Sigma project is accomplished in a team environment. Although the team concept at times contributes to a contentious experience, it ensures that the proper input is gathered at the appropriate times and from the appropriate resources. This practice greatly reduces the need for "over-the-fence" reviews. This practice is in stark contrast to the way that ISD is carried out. Although not explicitly stated, ISD supports an approach where the tasks accomplished in design are solely the responsibility of the instructional designer and done in isolation. The subsequent reviews and approvals of the outputs of this work are also done in isolation, with little or no context. The result all too often is a situation where there is a seemingly never-ending cycle of review, changes, and updates. This relationship leaves everyone involved in the process frustrated.

The second major difference between the two processes revolves around the tasks accomplished during the design phase. In ISD, the expectation is that the

FIGURE 8.2. DMADDI DESIGN ACTIVITIES.

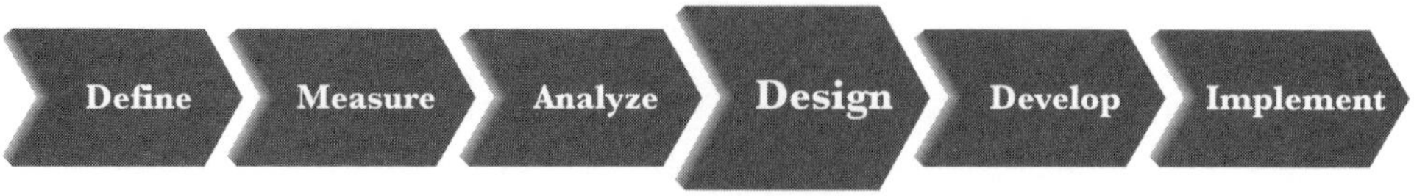

Define Measure Analyze **Design** Develop Implement

Objective	Activities	Tools	Deliverables
To specify how the tasks identified in analyze are to be learned	Write objectives Develop test items Plan instruction Identify resources	Measurable verbs Performance agreement chart Bloom's taxonomy	Measurable objectives Instructional strategy Prototype specifications Design tollgate

learning objectives, sequence, performance tests, and resource requirements are all identified at this point in the process. In DMADDI the learning objectives and their sequence are determined during the analyze phase. The budget and time restrictions are identified in the define phase. Performance tests are created only if, during that phase, the business review team deems performance tests necessary. In addition, the success criteria for the project are identified during the measure phase.

Having these decisions made prior to the design phase relieves instructional designers of the burden of engaging in activities that are not essential competencies of their vocation and allows them to concentrate on the activities that they tend to be most comfortable engaging in: determining the appropriate learning platform and developing instructional strategies and methods. With DMADDI, instructional designers are free to focus on designing instructional strategies that ensure the learning requirements identified in the analyze phase are met. Thus, just as the analyze phase of DMADDI focused on the "what" (as in, "What needs to be learned?"), the design phase focuses on the how, as in, "How do we teach it?" The design phase is also where the resources required to construct or develop the training course are identified. Now that the differences in the design phase of both methodologies are clear (Table 8.1), let's look at what takes place in the design phase of DMADDI.

TABLE 8.1. COMPARISON OF THE DESIGN PHASE OF ISD AND DMADDI.

ISD	DMADDI
Develop the learning objectives for each task.	Determine the learning platform.
Identify and list the learning steps required to perform the task.	Develop instructional strategies and methods.
Develop the performance tests to show mastery of the tasks to be trained.	Identify development resources.
List the entry behaviors that the learner must demonstrate prior to training.	
Sequence and structure the learning objectives, for example, do the easy tasks first.	

Design Step 1: Identify the Learning Platform

The first step in the design phase of DMADDI is to determine the appropriate learning platform or delivery option for the training solution. At this point in the project life cycle, the team knows what the business requirements are, they know the learning requirements, they are aware of any budget or time restrictions, and they should be versed on the demographic makeup of the target audience. This information is the basis for choosing the appropriate delivery platform for the training program. One tool that can be useful in ensuring that this decision is made based on the facts and not office politics is a decision matrix. Developing a decision matrix is largely a matter of listing the major factors that will affect the training program and classifying them (for example, as long or short, or high or low). Once the matrix has been completed, the team can map the results to the appropriate learning platform or delivery option.

Developing a Decision Matrix

There are essentially two steps to developing a decision matrix. The first step is to categorize the classifications. The reason that the classifications must be categorized is that there is no universal definition for most of the classifications. For example is $50,000 considered a large budget or a small budget? Are five thousand employees a large number to train or a small number to train? Is eight months a long duration or a short duration? There are no universal answers for these types of issues. It is therefore important that the team arrive at a collective understanding of these classifications based on the situation.

Once the classifications have been assigned, the team will be positioned to map their unique situation. The results of the mapping determine the delivery option. One technique that can be used categorize the classifications is the graphing technique. The exercise to categorize the various classifications might happen like this.

Let's say that the delivery team is in a meeting where the purpose is to determine the correct delivery option for the accounting program. The team facilitator leads the team through an exercise designed to get agreement on how to categorize each of the classifications. The facilitator puts three boxes on a conference table labeled "Low," "Medium," and "High." The facilitator then states, "We need to get an understanding on what constitutes a low, medium, or high budget." The team members are asked to write down their opinions on each and put their responses in the appropriate box.

This exercise takes place with no discussion. Many times in team situations that use debate as the mode of decision making, the best debater almost always wins. But just because someone is a good at arguing their point doesn't mean that he or she is correct. This technique for getting opinions reduces debate, maximizes input from all team members, and reduces contention.

Once all of the team members have placed their thoughts into the appropriate boxes, the facilitator asks for two volunteers: one to read the responses and the other to place the responses on a sheet of graph paper. Starting with the "High" budget box, the first volunteer reads the responses, $250,000, $150,000, $150,000, and $180,000. The responses that are identified as high budget might be written in red. Next, the facilitator asks the first volunteer to read the responses from the "Low" budget box. The responses are $5,000, $50,000, $20,000, and $15,000. These responses are represented on the graph with green markers. Finally, the facilitator asks for the responses from the "Medium" box to be read. This time the responses are $100,000, $80,000, $125,000, and $60,000. These responses are added to the graph, this time with blue marker.

The facilitator now points out to the team that based on the input from all team members, a high budget is considered as falling between $150,000 and $250,000, a medium budget is between $60,000 and $125,000, and a small budget is between $5,000 and $50,000. This graphing technique has allowed the team to get agreement on the characteristics of the budget with no arguments, no contention, and no time wasted in debate. This same technique should be repeated for each of the other classifications that the team is attempting to get agreement on. Once that is complete, the team has some objective criteria by which to map the characteristics of the project that they are working on.

Assembling the Matrix

With the classification correctly categorized, a decision matrix can be assembled by using the approved classifications. The team must now fill in the matrix based on two factors: (1) the criteria for the classifications that were identified using the graphing technique and (2) the specific conditions that the team is faced with. In the measure phase, for example, the maximum budget for this project was identified as $110,000. According to what the team agreed to with graphing, this would be considered a medium budget. Each of the other factors would also be labeled appropriately in the matrix. For example, the program must be completed in eight months. That factor would be appropriately plugged into the matrix based on how the team agreed that an eight-month project should be classified. There are one hundred employees to be trained. This factor would be classified and labeled in the matrix appropriately. Once all of the factors have been correctly added to the matrix, the appropriate delivery option will be decided.

Why the Delivery Solution Is Being Identified in the Design Phase

At this point training professionals who are versed in ISD might be questioning the wisdom of identifying the delivery solution during the design phase of the process. According to DMADDI, the analyze phase is where "what" needs to be learned is identified. Design is where the "how" is addressed, and the delivery platform is a component of "how." It answers the question, "How will we deliver the solution?" Therefore, this decision should be made during the design phase. In addition, how it will be delivered directly affects how it will be taught. In other words, the delivery platform directly affects the decisions around the learning activities that will be used.

Design Step 2: Convert Objectives into Learning Activities

Now that the team has identified the platform that will be used to deliver the learning solution, it can focus on creating learning activities. This is the point in the process when the instructional designer exerts more of a leadership role. In addition, an understanding of adult learning principles and Gagné's nine components of instruction come into play. If the delivery platform is a Web-based solution, the instructional designer should be familiar enough with the capabilities of the various platforms to provide leadership in that area too. The other members of the design team have important roles as well: they must assist in making sure the learning activities that are selected allow the project to continue to meet the business requirements.

In order to convert the learning objectives into learning activities, the team might consider continuing the use of a Six Sigma tool that might have been used previously, quality functional deployment (QFD).

More About QFD

We first learned about QFD in Chapter Five as a tool to assist in converting business requirements into measurable targets. In fact, it has a larger role. It can be used early in any development project to align and focus the development team. It can also be used as a tool to assist in planning and organizing requirements throughout the design and development of a project, and it is also a process that ensures that the voice of the customer drives the entire development process. QFD was originally developed to bring a personal interface to business. In today's training world, there is a growing distance between the concerns of the producers of the training and the concerns of those who pay for it. QFD links the needs of the customer (that is, the end user) with the design and development of the training program. It helps organizations seek out both the spoken and unspoken needs and translate them into actions and designs.

Quality Functional Deployment (QFD)

QFD is a set of powerful product development tools developed in Japan to transfer the concepts of quality control from the manufacturing process into the new product development process. The main features of QFD are a focus on meeting market needs by using actual customer statements, that is, the voice of the customer, its effective application of multidisciplinary teamwork, and the use of a comprehensive matrix, called the *house of quality,* for documenting information, perceptions, and decisions. Some of the benefits of adopting QFD have been documented as:

- Reduced time to market
- Fewer design changes
- Decreased design and manufacturing costs
- Improved quality
- Increased customer satisfaction

History of QFD

QFD was developed in Japan in the late 1960s at a time when statistical quality control had taken root in the Japanese manufacturing industry. Joseph M. Juran, Kaoru Ishikawa, Mitchell J. Feigenbaum, and other notable scholars emphasized the importance of making quality control a part of business management.

This mind-set was built on by Shigeru Mizuno and Yoji Akao, who developed a quality assurance method that would design customer satisfaction into a product before it was developed. Prior quality control methods were aimed primarily at fixing a problem during or after development.

In 1972, Katsuyoshi Ishihara introduced value engineering principles to describe how a product and its components work. He expanded this to describe business functions necessary to ensure the quality of the design process itself. Merged with these new ideas, QFD eventually became the comprehensive quality design system for both product and business processes.

The introduction of QFD to the United States and Europe began in 1983 when the American Society for Quality Control published Akao's work in *Quality*. Today QFD continues to inspire strong interest around the world, generating new applications, practitioners, and researchers each year. The application of QFD to training programs, however, remains a new and largely unexplored opportunity.

QFD Process

There are many different approaches to QFD. One four-phase approach uses a QFD matrix to translate customer wants into product specifications. The product specifications are then translated through another QFD matrix into design requirements. The design requirements are translated into design specifications. The design specifications become the success criteria. This four-phase approach is often referred to as the "Four Houses of Quality." Figure 8.3 is a visual representation of this approach.

FIGURE 8.3. FOUR HOUSES OF QUALITY.

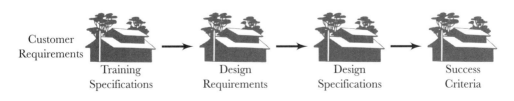

| Customer Requirements | Training Specifications | Design Requirements | Design Specifications | Success Criteria |

In the design phase of DMADDI, QFD is used as follows:

1. The learning objectives (grouped by category) are listed in Table 8.2 in the column labeled "learning objective."
2. Column 2 contains the importance (as determined during prioritization).
3. For each learning objective listed, the team must assign a learning activity.
4. Place an X in the cell where there is an intersection of a learning objective and a learning activity that will help the student meet that objective.

TABLE 8.2. QUALITY FUNCTIONAL DEPLOYMENT MATRIX.

Learning Objective/ Learning Activity	Importance	Simulation	Matching Table Exercise	Simulation	Simulation	Role play
Log on to System	2	X				
Check/Validate Reason Codes	4		X			
Forward Information to Supervisor	3			X		
Update Account Information	2				X	
Address Angry Customer	1					X

Design Step 3: Create a Communication Tool

Now that the learning objectives have been translated into learning activities, the next step in the design phase is to create a communication tool that will convey to those doing the development exactly what must be created. This includes visuals, flip charts, handouts, and simulations. If the deliver option for the training is some type of instructor-led training (either classroom based or Web based) the communication tool should be a lesson plan. If the delivery will be using an asynchronous or self-paced option, then the communication tool should be some form of a storyboard. (The storyboard that is used by the design team as a communication tool for developers who will be doing the work to develop the course is a different tool from the storyboard used to communicate project progress to stakeholders.)

Some believe that if the same person responsible for designing the course will also be developing and delivering the training, then there is less of a need to create these communication tools. This is not the case. If the original designer leaves the company or is away from the job for an extended period of time and no communication tool exists, it becomes virtually impossible for another individual to deliver the course or even complete the development of the course.

Some training organizations forgo the use of these communication tools. If the delivery option is some form of self-paced learning through the Internet, the proponents of rapid prototyping say there is no need for storyboards. In the case of instructor-led training, some organizations simply rely on the instructor's memorizing the content or the use of bullets in a PowerPoint presentation. The philosophy of DMADDI suggests that this is a dangerous practice that opens the door for the dreaded review-and-approval cycle.

The Lesson Plan

When the delivery option for the training program is instructor-led training, either classroom based or over the Internet, the tool that communicates what needs to be developed is the lesson plan. Although the lesson plan is not a Six Sigma tool, it is key in DMADDI because it is a mechanism that connects the design and the development phases of the process.

A lesson plan is a detailed blueprint for presenting training by an instructor. It prevents training from becoming haphazard and provides for training standardization. It is built on the lesson outline and includes all the details required for the presentation. It must have sufficient detail that a new instructor can teach the lesson with no training. It is a written guide for trainers and provides specific definition and direction on learning objectives, equipment, instructional media material requirements, and conduct of the training.

Components of a Lesson Plan. Although there are many variations in lesson plan designs, all contain some common characteristics. A good plan includes each of Gagné's nine components of instruction. A considerable amount of time should be spent on planning the lesson plan. This work will decrease the time the instructor needs to become more familiar with the content and also reduces the back-and-forth communication that will take place with the individuals responsible for developing the instructional materials. Good planning can prevent many problems.

Following are the basic components of a lesson plan:

- The topic: A statement of what is going to be covered—a designation of what area of content, facts, and issues the lesson will deal with.

- Audience and prerequisites: Who the lesson is for and what prior knowledge, skills, and attitudes those learners need for the lesson.
- Goals and objectives: A list of the learning outcomes expected as a result of the lesson. This section includes a discussion of how the lesson supports the larger curriculum.
- Instructional plan: Describes the activities that the learners will engage in and the sequence of those activities. It also describes what the instructor is going to do to facilitate those activities.
- Materials: A list of the materials necessary for successfully teaching the lesson. It includes a list of any Web pages that will be visited, flip charts required, and handouts. It also includes the actual materials (worksheets and Web pages) that must be prepared by the developer, any special requirements for classroom setup and supplies, and a list of specific hardware and software requirements.
- Plans for assessment and evaluation: A plan for assessing learning and evaluating the lesson as a whole. It may include a description of a model project, sample exam questions, or other elements of assessment. It also should include a plan for evaluating the lesson as a whole, including feedback from learners.

Approving Lesson Plans. Once the lesson plan is complete, the entire design team must officially approve it. This approval is critical: required course materials cannot be developed until the plan is approved. Once again with DMADDI, the process of getting approval for the lesson plan is slightly different from the traditional approach. With traditional methodologies, there tends to be a considerable back-and-forth review and update process that takes place in order to get lesson plans approved. With DMADDI, much of the back and forth is eliminated because the major components of the lesson plan have already been agreed to by the team as a result of the team collaboration that has taken place throughout the process. The learning activities, for example, are already agreed to, as is the sequencing of the content.

A variety of techniques can be used to get approval for the lesson plan, including consensus or majority vote. The team, however, should have set up rules by which they will make decisions at the time that the charter was developed. Whatever that method was should be applied to approving the storyboard.

Some might argue that the responsibility for the lesson plan belongs with the designer. The reality, however, is that the department or individuals commissioning the training will have something to say about the content and how it is taught. Including them in the process builds goodwill and knocks down many political barriers.

The Storyboard

A second tool that can be used to communicate design requirements to a developer is the storyboard. This storyboard, however, is different from the Six Sigma storyboard used to communicate project status to stakeholders.

Like the lesson plan, this storyboard is not a Six Sigma tool. It is key in DMADDI because, like the lesson plan, it is a mechanism that connects the design and the development phases of the process, and the handoff from design to development is one of the most critical transitions in the development of self-paced training programs. If the delivery option for the learning program is going to be a self-paced program delivered over the Internet, the storyboard is the appropriate communication tool. Storyboards can ensure that this is a smooth process and that the output that the design team envisioned is what is ultimately delivered. Without this communication tool, work must often be redone. In the process, budgets and schedules are often missed, and the final product is not everything the design team intended.

Components of a Storyboard. The storyboard is a screen-by-screen description of what students will see, hear, and do during the training program. The designer leads the development of this road map. The storyboard then becomes the guidebook for any artists, audio and video producers, and programmers who might be involved with the development of the training program. Storyboards provide a complete picture of what the final training program will look like. They use sketches or clip art to depict required art elements. The look and feel of a training storyboard might differ from organization to organization; however, every storyboard should have the following eight major elements.

Project Information. The information includes the name of the client; the curriculum title; the course title, date, draft, or version number; and script page number.

Screen Label. The screen label indicates which screen of the program is being described. (Sometimes screens are called *events, scenes,* or *frames.*) These screen labels should be coded with the lesson number and a screen number. For example, Screen 02–007 refers to lesson 2, screen 7. Some practitioners put an extra zero at the end of the screen counter to leave room to fit additional screens into the script in the future. For example if there were a need to add a new screen in lesson 6 between the existing screens 12 and 13, the revised script would reference the new screen as "06–0125." This labeling system can save a lot of time and energy later. Since artists name graphical images using these numerical screen labels as file names, this system avoids the need to renumber all the screens in the script whenever a new page is added.

Audio/Narration. This is specified in the script only if the technology used supports it. Typically an audio voice over (sometimes labeled *VO* in the script) of the narrator is used. Sometimes the audio segment of a script specifies "Play dramatic music," "Buzzer sound on incorrect answer," or some other sound effect.

Video Clips. If video clips are used, they are typically described in the script in a way that gives the camera direction and writes out the actual dialogue for on-screen actors. Descriptive notes to the director might be included—for example, "executive at her desk," "prestigious environment," or "slow zoom as she reaches her conclusion."

Graphics. Graphics are provided in the script as a verbal description of what should appear on screen or a sketch. They help both the reviewer (the client or a subject matter expert) and the artist who must create the final images to visualize what the designer has in mind. Descriptions might be specific, for example, "Show group of businesspeople around a conference table, gender balanced and multiculturally diverse," or vaguer, for example, "Computer on desk." General descriptions enable artists to apply their own creativity and resources. However, given only a loose interpretation, the final graphic the artist creates may not match what the designer had in mind.

On-Screen Text Section. The script that describes which words will appear on the screen should also be included. In many Web-based training programs that cannot support audio, text is the primary learning medium; therefore, this section of each script page may be quite long. In programs where audio narration is the primary instructional media, the text is used to reinforce the audio. In these cases, the text is likely to appear as brief bulleted points or short statements.

Navigation and Interactivity. Navigation describes the action items of the program, such as what the student can do on the screen and what will happen next. Standard navigation options include phrases such as, "Next button moves to next screen in sequence" and "Menu button jumps back to Main Menu." These types of options that are available from every screen often are excluded from the description. Once noted on the first script page, navigation is assumed to be constant. Other types of interactivity might be, "Answer A: Play buzzer sound and display in feedback window, 'That's incorrect. Try again,'" or directions can be related to the theme or metaphor, for example, "Clicking elevator doors causes doors to open, followed by interior elevator scene, and movement to fifth floor (lesson five)."

Notes. This final section in a script provides an area for any comments that do not fit easily into one of the other categories. This area allows the designer to communicate directly to an artist or programmer. Comments might be: "The corporate culture is very conservative. Let's make this opening screen reflect that. Feel free to get creative!" or, "This question segment needs to be tracked for final report purposes. We need to track specific answers in addition to correct and incorrect information."

Approving Storyboards. Once the storyboard is complete, the entire design team must officially approve it. This approval is critical since even small wording revisions in audio narration or video segments will require rehiring and scheduling actors and voice talent, additional time in a studio or recording booth, and the digitizing and editing of sequences. As with approving lesson plans, the DMADDI methodology reduces the review-and-approval cycle as a result of the team collaboration that has taken place in order to create the storyboard. The fact that the appropriate stakeholders are on the design team and have contributed in developing the storyboard reduces the rework opportunity.

Design Step 4: Identify Development Resources

At this point in design, the team is aware of the delivery option. It knows what learning activities will take place in the course and thus what needs to be developed. The team is now positioned to identify the resources required to develop the actual course. Obtaining the resources is normally not a problem since the training manager is part of the business review team. The design team might, however, be inclined to do a build-versus-buy analysis. The final decision should be based on the ability of each of the options to comply with the business targets for the project.

Design Step 5: Complete the Design Tollgate

As was the case in the analyze phase, in the design tollgate, members of the design team will be reporting their findings to the business review team and the project sponsor. This formal presentation should also be facilitated by the project leader, and each member of the design team should have a role. Prior to the toll-gate, the team should be diligent in completing the design checklist and prepare and practice for the presentation. The project storyboard should be updated, and team members should spend time validating how their findings will affect the business requirements of the project.

EXHIBIT 8.1. DMADDI DESIGN CHECKLIST.

Instructions: Respond appropriately to the following questions.

1. Have the design team members agreed on the delivery solution?	
2. Have the design team members agreed on the learning activities?	
3. Has a storyboard or lesson plan been completed?	
Comments:	
Team Member Signatures:	

DMADDI Tools for Design

Lesson Plan

Purpose: To demonstrate all of the components required for an instructor-led course

When to Use

• In the design phase

EXHIBIT 8.2. LESSON PLAN: RECONCILING ACCOUNTS RECEIVABLE.

Instructor: John Doe	Time: 1 hour	Date:10/30/06
Topic	Accounting Compliance	
Audience	Clerical Workers Grade 44	
Goals and objectives	Students will list the ten federal rule changes.	
	Students will describe how each of the new rules affect their current job.	
Instructional Plan		
Review	Discuss key points from the previous lesson. This will be done through question and answers.	
Preparation	There will be a sentence on the whiteboard that asks each student to write as many federal rules as they can think of. (5 minutes)	
Input and modeling	Explain the lesson: To find three important implications about the changes to a reason code and to present the findings to the class.	
	Demonstrate: How to access the material on the Internet.	
	How to input information into PowerPoint.	
	Access: End the modeling through a question and answer to check for understanding.	
Guided practice	Each student will be assigned three reason codes.	
	Students will use the Internet to identify three implications.	
	Students will input findings into PowerPoint.	
	Students will present findings to class.	
Closure	Review reasons for the rule changes by calling on students.	
	Review proper research methods.	
	Discuss the importance of using PowerPoint as a presentation tool.	
Independent practice	Students research and input three additional reason codes.	
Materials	Computers	
	PowerPoint	
	Sample reason code list	
	Internet access	

Steps to Follow:

1. As a team, complete all components of the template.
2. Get sign-off from all team members.

Storyboard

Purpose: To demonstrate all of the components required for an asynchronous course

When to Use

- In the design phase

Steps to Follow:

1. As a team, complete all components of the template.
2. Get sign-off from all team members.

Summary

This chapter concentrated on the design phase of DMADDI, when the question, "How do we teach it?" is answered. The work and focus of this phase remain with the design team, and the business review team continues in its role as the oversight committee. This chapter explained the differences that exist in the design phase of DMADDI and the design phase of ISD, walked through the steps required to complete the design phase of DMADDI, and presented some Six Sigma tools that are useful in this endeavor.

CHAPTER NINE

DEVELOP

Does Our Prototype Match Our Design?

In the develop phase of DMADDI, the training course is constructed. The work to develop the course materials is completed by the appropriate authors and multimedia and graphic production resources, and directly overseen by the instructional designer. The design team simultaneously continues its work by using Six Sigma tools that will help to validate that the output of the develop phase will meet the business targets set by the business review team. This chapter continues to focus on the Six Sigma tools that are useful in assisting the team to complete this phase.

DMADDI Road Map

Develop is the phase of a training development project where many who are involved get the most enjoyment. It is the conduit by which the design of a course and the implementation of a course are connected. Many instructional designers find this the most rewarding phase of a training project because it is where they get to see everything come to fruition. In the DMADDI model, develop is the phase where a prototype is created and the design team answers the question, "Does our prototype match our design?" (Figure 9.1).

FIGURE 9.1. DMADDI ROAD MAP FOR DEVELOP.

Define — What are the business requirements?

Measure — What targets do we need to meet?

Analyze — What needs to be learned?

Design — How should we teach it?

Develop — Does our prototype match our design?

Implement — Did the implementation meet business and instructional requirements?

Develop in ISD

In ISD, the objective of the develop phase is to produce the instructional materials that will be used in the training program—typically course materials, learning activities, lesson plan, leader's guide tests, and other assessment materials. Also, activities such as working with authors, flowcharting the course, and producing workbooks take place. Since training development is no longer limited to print materials and stand-up training in a classroom, instructional designers consider producing audio, video, computer-based, and Web-based course materials. Among the delivery options are computer platforms, distance learning networks, intranets, the Internet, and a host of others. According to ISD, the tools typically used in this phase include authoring and multimedia packages as well as word processors. Typical outputs tend to be the workbooks and exercises. In the case of e-delivery, the outputs might include storyboards or completed electronic courses.

Develop in DMADDI

The develop phase in DMADDI (Figure 9.2) is marginally different from the same phase in ISD. Many of the activities are exactly the same: workbooks and exercises are created in both models, and electronic courses are developed. In DMADDI, however, learning activities and materials such as lesson plans and storyboards are created during the design phase. In DMADDI the delivery option has already been determined by the time the team gets to this point.

FIGURE 9.2. DMADDI DEVELOP ACTIVITIES.

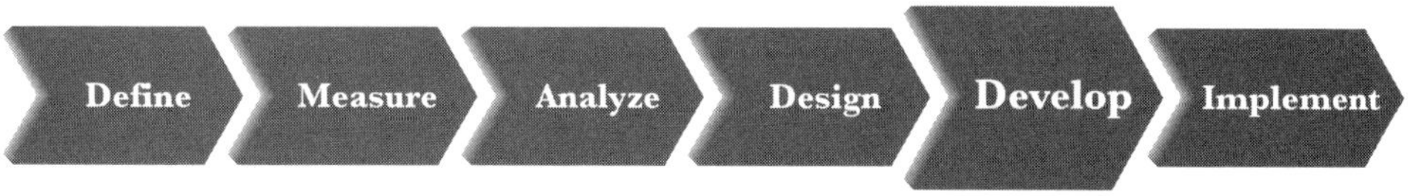

Define ▸ Measure ▸ Analyze ▸ Design ▸ **Develop** ▸ Implement

Objective	Activities	Tools	Deliverables
To author and produce instructional materials	Work with producers Develop workbooks Flowchart program Author content	Authoring tools Word processor Multimedia tools	Storyboard Script Exercises Computer-assisted instruction Develop tollgate

Perhaps the most noticeable difference between the two methodologies in this phase is that in order to prepare for implementation and to position the team to answer the question, "Does our prototype match our design?" DMADDI incorporates two important Six Sigma tools to validate that the outputs from the develop phase are positioned to ensure that the final deliverable meets the requirements been identified for the program. The tools that we focus on in this chapter are the Ishikawa diagram and the design failure mode and affect diagram.

In DMADDI, as the development is being completed by the appropriate authors, graphic artists, and multimedia programmers, the design team continues its work by setting up a system to validate that the outputs from this phase will meet the targets set by the business review team. The design team accomplishes this task by identifying factors that could possibly prevent the course from meeting its targets and then putting in place controls to prevent those events from occurring. The team then validates that the outputs of the develop phase match what was agreed to in design.

Develop Step 1: Identifying the Factors

The first task that the design team must undertake in the develop phase of DMADDI is to identify factors that could prevent the project from meeting its stated targets. Up to this point, the project has been through a series of tollgates that validated that the project is on target to meet the business goals. It is in the develop phase, however, that the rubber meets the road. The project is closer to completion and there is less time to recover from missed steps. The team must therefore be aware of any factors that could occur and take the project off target and have a plan in place for preventing any of these factors from occurring.

Ishikawa Diagram

One brainstorming tool that is helpful in identifying the factors is the Ishikawa diagram, the creation of Kaoru Ishikawa, a Japanese quality control statistician, who pioneered quality management processes in Japan's Kawasaki shipyards and in the process became one of the founding fathers of modern management.

The Ishikawa diagram is an analysis tool that provides a systematic way of looking at effects and the causes that create or contribute to those effects. It is often referred to as a cause-and-effect diagram. The Ishikawa diagram is also frequently referred to as the fishbone diagram because when it is drawn, it resembles the skeleton of a fish (Figure 9.3). The diagram is generally used to explore all the potential or real causes (or inputs) that result in a single effect (or output). In DMADDI, the team is attempting to identify any potential causes that might result in the course's not meeting business requirements. The causes are arranged in the diagram according to their level of importance or detail to depict relationships and a hierarchy of events. This tool helps the team search for root causes, identify areas where there may be problems, and compare the relative importance of different causes.

FIGURE 9.3. ISHIKAWA DIAGRAM.

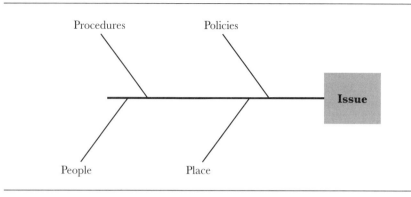

Procedures   Policies

Issue

People   Place

Constructing the Fishbone Diagram

The spine of the Ishikawa diagram represents the issue that the team is trying to address. The issues should be written in the form of a question. The causes are attached to the spine of the diagram like the bones of a fish. The common practice is to arrange the causes in four major categories. These categories can represent anything that makes sense for the specific project; however, for manufacturing projects, the categories tend to be staffing, methods, materials, and machinery, and for service projects place, policies, procedures, and people. These guidelines can be helpful but should not be used if they limit the diagram or are inappropriate.

Here are the basic steps that a team follows to build an Ishikawa diagram:

1. Draw the fishbone diagram.
2. List the problem or issue to be studied in the "head" of the fish.
3. Label each "bone" of the fish—for example, "Methods," "Machines," "Materials," and "Manpower" or "Place," "Procedure," "People," and "Policies."
4. Use an idea-generating technique to identify the factors within each category that may be affecting the problem or issue and effect being studied, or simply identify factors and then place them in the appropriate category. (Some factors may appear under more than one category.)
5. Continue until the team is no longer generating useful information.
6. Analyze the results of the fishbone after team members agree that an adequate amount of detail has been provided under each major category.
7. Use a Pareto chart to identify the most likely causes, by either category or factor.

Constructing an Ishikawa Diagram in DMADDI

Developing an Ishikawa diagram in DMADDI is a team activity lead by the project leader, who begins the meeting by explaining the diagram and why the team will be using it. The lead then hands out yellow stickies to each of the design team members and draws the fishbone on a flip chart. At the head of the flip chart, the project leader writes, "What could prevent the prototype from meeting design specifications?" and then labels the four categories—for example, "place, people, procedures, and policies."

The project leader asks each of the team members to write down as many factors as they can think of on the stickies, with one factor per sticky. Having each team member write down their ideas reduces the tendency that most teams have to debate each idea that is offered. When the team leader notices that most of the team members have stopped writing, he or she asks the team to place their factors on the flip chart next to the corresponding category.

Once the fishbone has been populated, the team leader asks for a volunteer to read the factors that appear under each of the categories (one volunteer for each category). After all of the factors have been read, the team can apply the CDAM technique to add any factors that were missed, combine factors that were written differently but have the same meaning, delete factors that appear not to apply, and modify the wording of any factors that require it.

Develop Step 2: Developing Controls

With the Ishikawa diagram complete and the potential factors identified, the team has several options for choosing which factors it wants to address. It also has several options for developing strategies to prevent those factors from occurring. One is to use a combination of the Pareto chart and the random word technique. If the team decided to use these tools, it would enter the data from the fishbone into a Pareto chart. This would identify for the team either the category or the factors that appeared to be the most likely to occur. The team would then use the random word technique to generate solutions for preventing the factors from occurring.

Another Six Sigma tool that can be useful in identifying what factors to address and developing strategies to ensure that they do not occur is failure mode effects analysis (FMEA), a disciplined approach used to identify possible failures of a product or service and then determine the frequency and impact of the failure. It is also used to rank and prioritize the possible causes of failures, as well as develop and implement preventative actions, with responsible persons assigned to carry out these actions.

FMEAs have been around for a long time. Before there was any documented format, process experts would try to anticipate what could go wrong with a design or process before it was developed. This method was used because trial and error was too costly and time-consuming. FMEAs were introduced in the late 1940s and were helpful in avoiding errors on small sample sizes of costly rocket technology. Use of the FMEA was encouraged in the 1960s for space product development and served well on getting a man on the moon. The Ford Motor Company reintroduced FMEA in the late 1970s for safety and regulatory consideration after the disastrous Pinto affair. It also used FMEAs effectively for production and design improvement.

In lay terms, FMEA is a structured technique to analyze a design or a process to determine shortcomings and opportunities for improvement. By assessing the severity of a potential failure, the likelihood that the failure will occur, and the chance of detecting the failure, dozens or even hundreds of potential issues can be prioritized for improvement. The FMEA is crucial to assessing the risk of product failure and devising focused actions to reduce that risk. The FMEA is the result of a design team's review of their product's functionality and characteristics.

Although training programs require many of the same activities as manufacturing products, they are actually quite different. The DMADDI methodology strongly recommends that an FMEA be completed in order to identify potential failures. The same rigor that is necessary when completing an FMEA for a new car design, for example, is not required for a training program. Therefore, while essentially the same process is followed in completing an FMEA for a training design project or for an automotive design project, the type of FMEA done for a training design project using DMADDI is slightly modified. Some of the more painstaking mathematical calculations that are required in producing a defect-free automobile are not practical to apply when developing training programs.

In DMADDI projects, the team is attempting to analyze the potential factors that may occur, as identified by using the fishbone technique. The team then assesses the severity of the results if these factors occur, the probability or likelihood that they will occur, and the ability of the team to detect the occurrences. The outputs of this process are a prioritized list of the factors that pose the greatest risk to this phase of the project and recommended actions to prevent these factors from occurring. When performed with good discipline and appropriate timing, the FMEA is the proverbial ounce of prevention.

How FMEA Is Completed in DMADDI

As with most of the other activities that take place in the DMADDI model, the FMEA is a team exercise. Since the FMEA is another Six Sigma tool, the activity would be led by the project or team leader, who is a Green Belt or Black Belt. As was the case with the Ishikawa diagram, the project leader begins by explaining what the team is attempting to accomplish and what tool they will be using. Prior to the meeting, the team leader should have had a volunteer draw a facsimile of Exhibit 9.1 on a whiteboard in the meeting room and now direct the team's attention to the chart.

EXHIBIT 9.1. MODIFIED FAILURE MODE AND EFFECTS ANALYSIS.

Project Name: Accounting Training

P = Probabilities (chance) of Occurrences
S = Seriousness of Failure
D = Ability to Detect
R = Risk Priority Measure (P × S × D)

Final Design: 15/06/2006
Prepared by:

Reviewed by: Chris
FMEA Date (Org.): 27/04/2006

1 = very low or none   2 = low or minor   3 = moderate or significant   4 = high   5 = very high or catastrophic

No.	Factor	Cause(s) of Failure	Effect(s) of Failure	Current Control	P	S	D	R	Recommended Corrective Action(s)
					P.R.A.				
1	Wrong learning objectives	Incorrect analysis	Noncompliance	Team review tollgate	1	4	1	4	NA
2	Prototype doesn't match design	Incorrect storyboard	Rework, missed deadline, over budget	Team review tollgate	1	4	1	4	NA
		Misinterpretation of storyboard	Rework, missed deadline, over budget	NA	2	4	2	16	Checkpoint meetings with developers
3									

The "Factor" column can be prepopulated with the factors that were identified using the fishbone diagram, or the facilitator can elicit the findings of the fishbone from the team after their attention has been drawn to the chart. The next step in the process is to elicit from the team the causes of failure, or the reasons that the first factor might occur. The leader would then elicit from the team what effect the failure would have on the project. After that, the team would determine what control is currently in place to prevent the failure from occurring. The next step is for the team to calculate the risk priority measure by assigning a numerical value to the probability that a factor will occur, the seriousness of the factor should it occur, and the ability of the team to detect or prevent the factor from occurring.

These numbers are multiplied, and the result is the priority risk measure, which prioritizes for the team which factors to address. The higher the priority risk measure, the more important it is to address. Identifying the priority risk measure occurs as follows (the steps are summarized in Table 9.1):

1. The team assigns a numerical value to the probability that the factor will occur (P) on a scale of 1 (a very low or virtually no possibility that the factor will occur) to 5 (a very high probability that the factor will occur).

TABLE 9.1. STEPS TO COMPLETE FAILURE MODE AND EFFECTS ANALYSIS.

Step	Action
1.	Draw a facsimile of the FMEA chart on a whiteboard.
2.	List all factors in the "factor" column.
3.	Elicit the "causes of failure" or the reasons that the first factor might occur.
4.	Elicit from the team what effect the failure would have on the project.
5.	Determine what control is currently in place to prevent the failure from occurring.
6.	Assign a numerical value to the probability of a factor occurring (P).
7.	Assign a numerical value to the seriousness of the factor (S).
8.	Assign a numerical value to the ability of the team to detect or prevent the factor from occurring (D).
9.	Multiply the results (P $\times$ S $\times$ D).
10.	Recommend an action if the priority risk measure is high.
11.	Repeat for each factor.

2. The team assigns a numerical value to the seriousness of the factor should it occur (S), again on a scale of 1 (low impact or seriousness) to 5 (a high degree of seriousness or a catastrophic impact on the project's ability to meet its targets).

3. The team assesses its current ability to detect or prevent the factor from occurring (D). If the team currently has a control in place and there is a high probability that it could catch or prevent the factor from occurring, it assigns a low number. If there is no control in place and a high probability that the team could not detect or prevent the factor from occurring, a high number is assigned.

4. The team multiplies these three factors ($P \times S \times D$) to arrive at the priority risk measure.

5. The team recommends an action if the priority risk measure is high.

This process is repeated for each of the factors that was generated by the fishbone diagram.

Common FMEA Mistakes

FMEA is one of the more advanced Six Sigma tools. And although it is comprehensive, it can also be challenging and time-consuming for the team to complete. Nevertheless, the results can be well worth the effort.

In order to get the maximum benefit from the FMEA effort, there are some common mistakes that must be avoided: failing to define the function being analyzed, not recognizing all potential failures, misapplying ranking scales, confusing failure modes with effects or failure modes with causes, and failing to develop recommended actions or recommending actions that are neither actionable nor ex-

---

FMEA Mistakes to Avoid

- Failure to define the function being analyzed
- Not recognizing all potential failures
- Misapplication of ranking scales
- Confusing failure modes with effects or failure modes with causes
- Failure to develop recommended actions
- Recommending actions that are neither actionable nor executable
- Applying occurrence and detection too optimistically
- Allowing the FMEA to turn into a design review

ecutable. Other common mistakes are applying occurrence and detection too optimistically and allowing the FMEA to turn into a design review.

Develop Step 3: Validating the Outputs of the Develop Phase

Regardless of the technique used in the first two steps of the develop phase (whether it was fishbone followed by FMEA or fishbone followed by Pareto and random word analysis), the results of these steps position the team to have a plan in place that prevents destructive factors from occurring and identify the most critical components of the prototype that must be validated before the product is given the green light to move to implementation.

Ideally the team should compare each of the outputs of the develop phase with its description from the lesson plan or the storyboard developed in the design phase. The FMEA or other Six Sigma tools, if used, will, however, focus the team's attention on the "vital few" items that must be checked as opposed to the "insignificant many." The team's time is better spent validating the factors that have a high probability of occurring, will have a serious impact on the project, and have a low probability of being detected previously than spending its time on factors that have a low probability of occurring, a minimal impact, and controls in place to detect the factor.

Develop Step 4: Complete the Develop Tollgate

In the tollgate, the members of the design team continue to report their findings to the business review team and the project sponsor. At this point in the process, the formal presentation can now be facilitated by a team member other than the project leader. The exposure and participation in the previous tollgates as well as the growing familiarity with the Six Sigma methodology, terminology, and tools by this time should have prepared all team members to take the lead in this high-level meeting. As with the other tollgates, each member of the design team should have a role. Prior to the tollgate review, the team should be diligent in completing the develop checklist (Exhibit 9.2) and prepare and practice for the presentation. If someone other than the project leader is going to facilitate the meeting, additional time should be spent preparing this person for the task. The project storyboard should be updated, and team members should spend time validating among themselves how their findings will affect the business requirements of the project.

EXHIBIT 9.2. DMADDI DEVELOP CHECKLIST.

Instructions: Respond appropriately to the following questions.

1. Have the design team members identified all potential factors that might affect project outcomes?	
2. Have the design team members validated that the prototype matches the approved design?	
3. Has the project storyboard been updated?	
4. Has the tollgate worksheet been completed?	
Comments:	
Team Member Signatures:	

DMADDI Tools for Develop

Ishikawa Diagram

FIGURE 9.4. ISHIKAWA DIAGRAM.

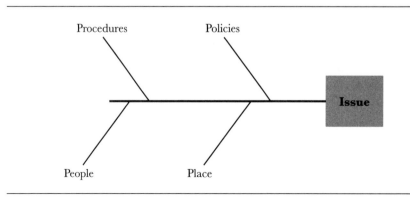

Purpose: To identify all of the factors that might affect the project's ability to meet business requirements

When to Use

- In the develop phase

Steps to Follow

1. Draw the fishbone on a flip chart.
2. At the head of the flip chart, write the issue in the form of a question.
3. Label the fishbone with four categories.
4. Hand each team member a package of sticky notes.
5. Have each team members write down as many factors as they can think of on the sticky notes that they have been given (one factor per sticky note).
6. Team members place their factors on the flip chart next to the corresponding category and then apply the CDAM technique.

Failure Mode Effects Analysis

Purpose: To identify the risk associated with factors that might affect a project's ability to meet business requirements

When to Use

- In the develop phase

Steps to Follow

1. Draw a facsimile of the FMEA chart on a whiteboard.
2. List all factors in the "factor" column.
3. Elicit the "causes of failure" or the reasons that the first factor might occur.
4. Determine what control is currently in place to prevent the failure from occurring.
5. Assign a numerical value to the probability of a factor occurring (P).
6. Assign a numerical value to the seriousness of the factor (S).
7. Assign a numerical value to the ability of the team to detect or prevent the factor from occurring (D).
8. Multiply the results $(P \times S \times D.)$
9. Recommend an action if the priority risk measure is high.
10. Repeat for each factor.

EXHIBIT 9.3. FAILURE MODE EFFECTS ANALYSIS.

Project Name: Accounting Training

P = Probabilities (chance) of Occurrences
S = Seriousness of Failure
D = Ability to Detect
R = Risk Priority Measure (P × S × D)

Final Design: 15/06/2006
Prepared by:

Reviewed by: Chris
FMEA Date (Org.): 27/04/2006

1 = very low or none 2 = low or minor 3 = moderate or significant 4 = high 5 = very high or catastrophic

No.	Factor	Cause(s) of Failure	Effect(s) of Failure	Current Control	P	S	D	R	Recommended Corrective Action(s)
							P.R.A.		
1	Wrong learning objectives	Incorrect analysis	Noncompliance	Team review tollgate	1	4	1	4	NA
2	Prototype doesn't match design	Incorrect storyboard	Rework, missed deadline, over budget	Team review tollgate	1	4	1	4	NA
		Misinterpretation of storyboard	Rework, missed deadline, over budget	NA	2	4	2	16	Checkpoint meetings with developers
3									

Summary

This chapter concentrated on the develop phase of DMADDI, when the question, "How do we teach it?" is answered. The work and focus of this phase remain with the design team, and the business review team continues in its role as the oversight committee. This chapter explained the differences in the design phase of DMADDI and the develop phase of ISD, walked through the steps required to complete the phase, and presented some of the Six Sigma tools that are useful in this endeavor.

CHAPTER TEN

IMPLEMENT

Did the Implementation Meet
Business and Instructional Requirements?

In the implement phase of DMADDI, the training program is introduced into a real-world environment. The focus of the project now shifts back to the business review team, which strives to validate that the result of the implementation (and, for that matter, the entire project) has addressed both the voice of the business and the voice of the customer. This chapter focuses on the Six Sigma tools that are useful in assisting the team in successfully completing the implement phase of DMADDI.

DMADDI Road Map

Implement is the only phase of a training development project that many of the project's stakeholders see. It is when the program that has taken weeks or months (and sometimes years) to design and develop is finally rolled out to the end user or student. It is the most visible component of the training program and, unfortunately as a result, too frequently the only component of the program that is evaluated. This evaluation (also unfortunately) traditionally takes place during a completely separate phase of the project. Depending on a stakeholder's role in the project, the implement phase could be the end or the beginning of his or her association with the project. Thus, for some of the stakeholders, implement is a new beginning, and for others it is a postmortem. As with ISD, this phase in the

DMADDI model is when the training program is inserted into the "real world." In DMADDI, however, the evaluation of this phase is not a separate activity. In DMADDI, the ultimate focus is to answer the question, "Did the implementation meet business and instructional requirements?" (Figure 10.1).

FIGURE 10.1. DMADDI IMPLEMENT ROAD MAP.

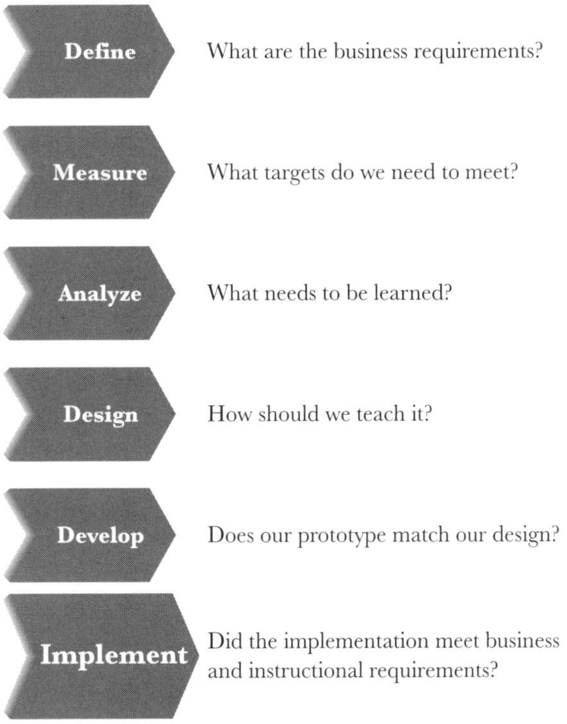

Define	What are the business requirements?
Measure	What targets do we need to meet?
Analyze	What needs to be learned?
Design	How should we teach it?
Develop	Does our prototype match our design?
Implement	Did the implementation meet business and instructional requirements?

Implement in ISD

Implementation in ISD is the presentation of the learning experiences to the targeted participants using the appropriate media. Depending on the source of reference, some suggest that the activities in this phase of ADDIE include pilot test, train the trainer, and course revisions. Others suggest that only full-scale production or full-scale delivery occurs in this phase and that course revisions are a result of the feedback gained during the evaluation phase of ADDIE. The instructional technology program at San Jose State suggests that teacher training and course pilots or tryouts take place in this phase of ISD and that the outputs of this phase include student data and comments. Whatever the source, however, there is no debate that the main focus of the implementation phase of ISD is to install the learning solution into a real-world context.

Implement in DMADDI

Implement in DMADDI (Figure 10.2) is different from the same phase in its ISD counterpart: it instead implements the solution to the target audience and validates that the solution has met the prescribed business and learning requirements.

FIGURE 10.2. DMADDI IMPLEMENT ACTIVITIES.

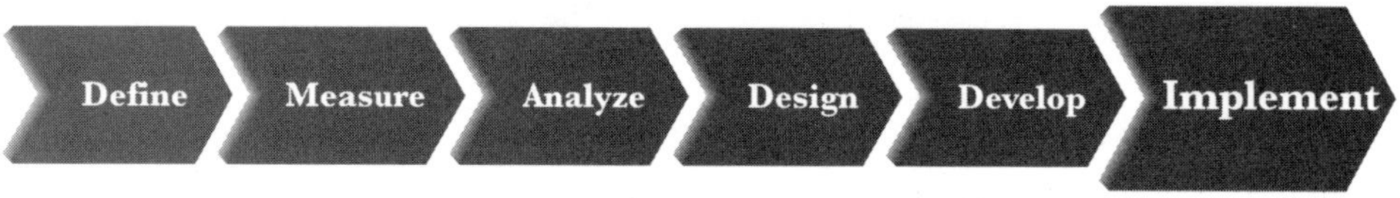

| Define | Measure | Analyze | Design | Develop | Implement |

Objective	Activities	Tools	Deliverables
To install the project in the real-world context	Teacher training Pilots	Management systems	Student comments Test data Implement tollgate

This focus has been built into the entire DMADDI process. It is evidenced across each of its phases and reinforced with tollgate reviews, governed by a project organization, and supported by a tool set geared to that end. There is no separate evaluation phase in the DMADDI process because evaluation is a formal component of every phase of the process. If DMADDI has been followed properly up to this point and the rigor of the methodology has been enforced, then the answer to the question, "Did the implementation meet both business and instructional requirements" is a forgone conclusion, and the outputs of the implement are largely a summary of the project work.

A Brief Recap

The define phase of DMADDI identified what was important to the business stakeholders of the project. The measure phase translated those "whats" into measurable targets for the project to meet. The analyze phase uncovered the learning requirements for the program. Thus, at the end of analyze, the project team had all of the requirements that would drive the project's metrics. At that point, the definition of the true return on investment for this project had been identified. With the analyze phase complete, the design team turned its attention to designing a learning solution that would meet all of the project specifications (both the business and learning specifications). Only after it was validated that the training product design met the training product specifications did the development of the training product begin. The completed product was tested to verify that it complied with or adhered to the design specifications.

The entire process has now brought the team to the point of installing the solution into the real world where the business review team must report on how well the product met the business and learning requirements identified during the first three phases of the project. This is the new measure of success and the true return on investment for training programs.

What Happens in the Implement Phase

The implement phase has two major focuses: to implement the learning solution to the target audience and to validate that the solution has met the prescribed business and learning requirements. The work to make the program available to its target audience is overseen by the training manager. The training manager or the training department has the resources, the expertise, and the experience in this area and is thus best suited to perform this function. The work to complete this function begins as soon as the project passes the develop tollgate. At the same time, the business review team begins its work to document the project's performance against project goals and present its findings to the project sponsor. The business review team is made up of individuals who have the expertise and experience in the business arena and are thus best suited to perform that function.

Although the work to compile the project data has been an ongoing process across the project life cycle and has been presented in various forms at the tollgates of each project phase, the timing for the final presentation of the findings is contingent on a few factors. The first are the requirements themselves. If, for example, for a given training project there is a business requirement to measure the feedback of all students who have completed the training, then the findings cannot be presented until all of those data have been gathered. If the business requirement is only that the development of the training meets a certain budget target, then the formal presentation can take place much earlier.

Most of the work to collect and analyze these data is done by the project leader, who has been trained in using the statistical tools of Six Sigma, and the individual in the project organization who has been the conduit for the entire project organization. Thus, the project leader is the right resource to perform this function. That being said, the most important factors for the project leader to consider in preparing for the final tollgate are the project's requirements and the perspective of the various stakeholders.

Analyzing and understanding these factors will help the project leader to determine the appropriate communication mode, the type of information to present, and the best means to present the report. As the project leader goes through this process, he or she should continue to use the techniques identified in the initial stakeholder analysis to ensure that all stakeholders in the process have the appropriate information prior to the formal presentation. There should be no surprises for anyone. Since there is no shortage of training books or articles that address the factors surrounding inserting a training project into a real-world environment, the focus here is on the work that takes place to answer the pivotal question associated with the implement phase. This is accomplished by revisiting the project requirements, validating the perspective of project stakeholders, gathering and analyzing project data, developing a reporting action plan, preparing a presentation, completing the final tollgate, and celebrating.

Implement Step 1: Revisit the Project Requirements

The business requirements for the training program have been constantly reviewed and referred to throughout the life cycle of the project. As the final tollgate nears, the project leader should continue to review these requirements and use them as a basis for decisions about the final presentation. He or she should review the project charter, the requirements worksheet (if one was used), any deployments that have been completed, previous phase tollgates, and checklists.

Implement Step 2: Validate the Perspective of the Stakeholders

As was the case with the business requirements, the perspective of the stakeholders has been monitored across the life cycle of the project. With the final presentation approaching, the project leader should review the stakeholder analysis form that was completed during the define phase. He or she should also take into account what he or she has learned about the stakeholders as the project interactions took place. Did a stakeholder start out requesting soft data but as the project went on start requesting more hard data? What are the business review team members interested in?

If none of the members of the business review team care about the learning requirements, does it make sense to report that information?

Implement Step 3: Gather and Analyze Project Data

Now that the project requirements been revisited and the perspective of the stakeholders have been revalidated, the team leader should gather the data that answer the questions that the stakeholders want addressed.

Implement Step 4: Develop a Reporting Action Plan

Once the project requirements have been revisited, the perspective of the stakeholders revalidated, and any project data collected have been analyzed, it is time to put together an action plan for the final presentation. Developing this action plan is a matter of creating a table that identifies each of the stakeholders and matching their concerns with the appropriate data required to address the concern (Table 10.1). The project leader should also consider if addressing an individual stakeholder's concerns requires continuous or discrete data. *Continuous data* refers to information that can be measured on a continuum or scale. This data can have almost any numerical value and can be meaningfully subdivided into finer and finer increments, depending on the precision of the measurement system. *Discrete data* refers to information that can be categorized into a classification. These data are based on counts. Only a finite number of values is possible, and the values cannot be subdivided meaningfully (for example, into good or bad, off or on, or yes or no).

TABLE 10.1. DMADDI REPORTING ACTION PLAN.

Stakeholder	Concern	Data Type	Supporting Data
Managing director	100 employees must complete the program within eight months	Discrete	All employees have completed the program. Program completed in seven months
Accounting manager	Program must cost less than $110,000 Employees must spend no more than four hours in training	Discrete	Program cost $80,000 Program length two and a half hours
Training manager	Wants to meet the business needs	Discrete	All business targets were met
CEO	Program must be completed within eight months	Discrete	Program completed in seven months
Accountants	No more than three hours spent in training	Discrete	Program length two and a half hours

Implement Step 5: Prepare Presentation and Update Storyboard

Once the reporting action plan has been completed, the project leader can begin to create the presentation and update the project storyboard. According to Table 10.1, all of the members of the business review team had requirements that could be reported with discrete data. From their collective perspectives, either the project met their requirements or it did not. This factor will affect the way the final data are presented to them. Prior to the formal and final tollgate, however, it would be wise for the project leader to "leak" the results to the team since there should be no surprises, good or bad.

As you can see from Table 10.2, none of the data to be reported to the business review team correspond with Kirkpatrick's four levels of evaluation. However, based on the requirements established by the team members, the training program would be considered successful. This model allows the team to present metrics that the project stakeholders find important, not data imposed by the training department.

TABLE 10.2. ACCOUNTING PROJECT METRICS TABLE.

Issue	Target	Actual	Target Met?
Budget	$110,000	$80,000	Yes
Project length	8 months	7 months	Yes
Seat time	3 hours	2.5 hours	Yes

Implement Step 6: Complete the Implement Tollgate

With the implement tollgate, all project team members should come together for the final project report, continuing to report their findings to the business review team and the project sponsor. The presentation should be facilitated by the project leader or (for political purposes) the managing director.

As many members of the project organization as possible should have a role in this meeting. Also, prior to the tollgate review, the team should be diligent in reviewing the presentation and completing the implement checklist (Exhibit 10.1)

EXHIBIT 10.1. DMADDI IMPLEMENT CHECKLIST.

Instructions: Respond appropriately to the following questions.

1. Have the project's requirements been validated?	
2. Have the project data been analyzed?	
3. Has an action plan been developed?	
4. Has the project storyboard been updated?	
5. Has the tollgate worksheet been completed?	

Comments:

Team Member Signatures:

Implement Step 7: Celebrate

Once the implement tollgate has been completed, the project leader should organize formal recognition for everyone in the project organization. A great perk would be if the project champion could attend the celebration and present the team members with some type of memento to thank them for their participation in the project.

A Final Word

Approaching a training program in the manner described exhibits that the training department not only has an understanding of business issues but also the ability to produce a program that addresses them. The partnership that takes place when a training manager is a member of a business review team together with the business stakeholders creates an atmosphere of goodwill that does not occur when the ISD approach to training development is used.

DMADDI Tools for Implement

DMADDI Action Plan

TABLE 10.3. DMADDI REPORTING ACTION PLAN.

Stakeholder	Concern	Data Type	Supporting Data
Managing director	100 employees must complete the program within eight months	Discrete	All employees have completed the program. Program completed in seven months
Accounting manager	Program must cost less than $110,000 Employees must spend no more than four hours in training	Discrete	Program cost $80,000 Program length two and a half hours
Training manager	Level assessments above 85 percent	Discrete	Pending
CEO	Program must be completed within eight months	Discrete	Program completed in seven months
Accountants	No more than three hours spent in training	Discrete	Program length two and a half hours

Purpose: To address stakeholder concerns with the appropriate data.

When to Use

• In the implement phase

Steps to Follow

1. List all stakeholders in column 1.
2. Add the appropriate concern next to each stakeholder.
3. Identify the data type associated with each concern.
4. List the data that supports the concern.
5. Vet with the team.
6. Distribute to stakeholders.

Summary

This chapter concentrated on the implement phase of DMADDI, where the question, "Did the implementation meet both business and instructional requirements?" is answered. In this phase, the training program is introduced into a real-world environment, and the focus of the project is shifted back to the business review team, which is charged with validating that the result of the implementation (and, for that matter, the entire project) has addressed both the voice of the business and the voice of the customer. The chapter explained the differences between the implement phase in DMADDI and the implementation phase of ISD, addressed a Six Sigma tool useful in this endeavor, and set out the steps required to complete the implement phase.

CHAPTER ELEVEN

IF NOT US, WHO? IF NOT NOW, WHEN?

A prizefighter enters the ring for the most important fight of his career. If he wins, he will be positioned as one of the top fighters in his weight class and will gain the respect of the entire boxing industry. In preparation for the battle, he has studied the style of his opponent and is aware that in order to win, he must use tactics that are different from his current approach to boxing. As the fight begins, the boxer starts off using the new tactics and is having success. As the fight progresses, however, the boxer regresses to his old style, and his opponent begins to get the better of him. At the end of each round, his handlers implore him to return to the tactics that have proven successful against this opponent. Finally, after several rounds of being pummeled, the boxer returns to his corner. Dazed and confused, he asks his handlers, "What is this guy doing?" His handlers look at him and respond, "It's not so much what he is doing to you as it is what you are refusing to do for yourself." The boxer ends up losing the match.

The story of this boxer is similar in many ways to the plight of too many training professionals. Training professionals are frequently presented with opportunities to win the respect of their business partners, only to thwart the opportunity by using tactics that are unable to translate the results of their programs into tangible business results. The think tanks of the training world continue to make the training professionals aware that to be successful in this arena, they must adjust the tactics that they are currently using and instead use business tactics. Many training professionals even begin their analysis by at least attempting to address business issues. As the process progresses, however, the lack of business tools and techniques available in the training tool kit causes the practitioners to revert to applying training approaches to business problems. This limited tool set gives them no resort but to return to the tactics that have never proven successful. This condition is in part the reason for the ambiguity that the executives who took the Accenture workforce survey reported (2004).

This book has given training professionals access to a tool set previously available only to quality or process improvement professionals. The chapters in Part One gave an overview of the issues facing training professionals. This was accomplished by first establishing what the instructional system design methodology is. Part One set out a brief history of ISD, identified the most popular ISD models and their methodologies, and discussed the strengths and weaknesses of ISD as it pertains to developing sound instruction and presenting business solutions. In fact, ISD is not equipped with any formal tools that are dedicated to identifying and quantifying business problems.

Chapter Two introduced training professionals to the Six Sigma methodology, pointing out that Six Sigma is a methodology with a proven track record of designing solutions that solve business problems. It gave a brief history of the philosophy and provided a good working definition of Six Sigma. It also explored two Six Sigma models and walked through the Six Sigma improvement and Six Sigma design methodologies. Chapter Three explored why it is essential for training professionals to adopt a business model as a development methodology for training programs. It accomplished this by exploring the business rationale for this paradigm shift and examining the shortcomings of ISD, explaining the benefits of a business approach. Finally, it presented DMADDI, a new development model for training programs.

The chapters in Part Two walked training professionals through the DMADDI model, in the process pointing out the similarities and the differences between the ISD and the Six Sigma approaches to designing training programs. These chapters explored a new tool set that can immediately be put into practice and presented scenarios that give a clear rationale for this new approach as well as some ideas on how to put the methodology into practice. The concept of the project champion, business review team, and the project organization were all introduced.

Part Three next presents a case study documenting the experience that one company had while applying the DMAIC or improvement Six Sigma methodology to its e-learning process. While the DMAIC or improvement methodology is slightly different from the DFSS or design approach, many of the tools are the same, and many of the team concepts are similar.

As a result of reading this book and applying some of the tools, techniques, and methodologies set out here, training professionals should now be better positioned to apply tactics that will prove successful at addressing both the voice of the customer and the voice of the business.

PART THREE

A DMAIC CASE STUDY

CHAPTER TWELVE

E-LEARNING THE SIX SIGMA WAY

A Case Study

What is the true cost of e-learning development? If a vendor develops your e-learning program, what additional costs are you incurring as a result of time spent reviewing and approving these products? What are the critical requirements of your e-learning customers? Are you meeting those requirements? What are the critical business imperatives that need to be addressed with the e-learning that you currently deliver? Are you meeting those imperatives? In articulating your e-learning vision, are you speaking a language that any business manager can understand?

If the answer to any of these questions is either "no" or "I don't know," your e-learning program may well be in trouble, and applying Six Sigma methodologies might be the solution to many of the problems that you are facing. Following is a case study detailing how the customer training department of the Depository Trust & Clearing Corporation (DTCC) applied Six Sigma methodologies to its e-learning development and as a result validated and exceeded critical customer and business requirements for e-learning, reduced e-learning development rework by 81 percent, reduced the annual cost of developing e-learning by 30 percent, and saved the company $282,000.

The Background

The Depository Trust & Clearing Corporation is the largest financial services post-trade infrastructure in the world, with operating facilities in multiple locations in the United States and overseas. With the company's growth, it was becoming more and more difficult for the customer training department to satisfy the increasing volume of customer training requests. A growing product line presented challenges in finding instructors who were certified on each of the products, and the need to rapidly deploy updated information was becoming more crucial. The leadership of the customer training department was convinced that e-learning would allow the company to satisfy its customer training requests, reduce the cost of training, and address the issue of trainer certification. Senior management was sold on the idea, an e-learning strategy was developed, and DTCC became one of the financial service industry's early adapters of e-learning.

Like many other training organizations, the customer training department spent significant money and resources researching and purchasing a learning management system (LMS), procuring a variety of authoring software packages, and training personnel to use the new software. Monies were allocated to teach training professionals how to develop and deliver e-learning. A benchmarking study was undertaken in order to ensure that the e-learning was "done right," a goal to convert all of the core instructor-led courses into self-paced electronic courses was set, a budget was established, a vendor was commissioned to assist with the project, and the e-learning journey began.

Two years into the program, concerns arose. Only two of the six core instructor-led courses had been converted for self-paced delivery. Two uncompleted courses had been in development for close to a year. The consulting budget that was set aside to convert the core courses was spent. The staff of the customer training department openly expressed frustration about the amount of time and rework associated with developing e-learning programs, the cost of e-learning development, and the quality of the e-learning that was being developed.

In order to address these issues, additional funds were invested to implement project management methodologies, certify staff as project management professionals, and improve the skills of the department's instructional designers. After some initial optimism with these measures, the frustration returned.

The leadership of customer training, which was still committed to fixing the e-learning "problems," volunteered to participate in the company's second round of Six Sigma projects. An initial project charter was developed, a cross-functional team was assembled, and the project began.

The Organizational Structure

To fully appreciate the challenges that the customer training Six Sigma Team faced, it is important to have an understanding of the structure of the organization as it pertained to e-learning. The customer training department is responsible for delivering training services to participants or customers of DTCC, which are financial industry firms. The end users of this training are the employees of these firms. Training requests came to customer training in one of three ways:

1. The member firm or participant would contact the relationship manager at DTCC with a training request. The relationship manager in turn would contact the customer training department.
2. Product management would identify a training need and then request that the customer training department develop a program.
3. The customer training department would examine trend analysis information from service desk calls and develop training based on those data.

In all three cases, however, the development costs of the e-learning were charged to the budget of the appropriate product manager, who ultimately had the authority to make decisions on content, look, and feel, as well as instructional strategies.

The customer training department itself was composed of four groups: the information product group, responsible for all customer documentation; the training group, responsible for delivery of all instructor-led programs; the project management group, responsible for delivering all customer training projects on time and within budget; and the instructional technologies group, responsible for e-learning development, instructional design, and LMS administration. A typical e-learning deliverable would require review, approval, and sign-off by all of these groups, as well as approval by product management.

What's Important? The Define Phase

The Six Sigma team started the project with some advantages. The customer training department's previous experience with project management provided some initial data. Many Six Sigma projects start with no analytical data whatsoever. At the project kickoff, the draft charter was distributed to team members, and the work began refining it and filling in the missing pieces. The initial data seemed to indicate tremendous opportunity to reduce rework, development time, and development cost. Rework accounted for up to 60 percent of the total development time. The development time was as much as 75 percent above the American Society of Training Directors (ASTD) benchmark of about two hundred hours of development time per hour of e-learning, and the development costs were affected by both rework and development time.

As the team worked on the charter, discussions arose around what the industry standard for e-learning consisted of and which benchmark to use. It was finally agreed that the ASTD would be the benchmark. The next point of discussion centered on the project's scope. After much debate, the team finally agreed that the scope of the project would be from the time a training need was identified until the e-learning deliverable was approved by product management. The team then agreed on a preliminary project plan with an activity schedule and some initial milestones.

Process Mapping

With the charter approved, the team focused its work on documenting and analyzing the e-learning development process as it currently existed. This was accomplished by developing a variety of maps and charts to give a graphical representation of what was really taking place in the e-learning development process. The first map that the team developed was a supplier, inputs, process, and output customer diagram (SIPOC). This diagram (Figure 12.1), with its few de-

FIGURE 12.1. SIPOC OF THE CUSTOMER TRAINING PROCESS.

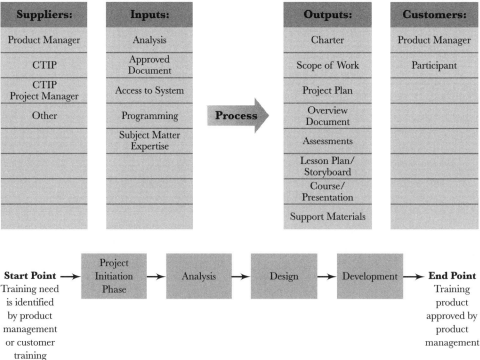

Customer Training and Information Products (CTIP) Process

Suppliers:	Inputs:		Outputs:	Customers:
Product Manager	Analysis		Charter	Product Manager
CTIP	Approved Document		Scope of Work	Participant
CTIP Project Manager	Access to System		Project Plan	
Other	Programming	**Process** ➤	Overview Document	
	Subject Matter Expertise		Assessments	
			Lesson Plan/ Storyboard	
			Course/ Presentation	
			Support Materials	

Start Point ➤ Project Initiation Phase ➤ Analysis ➤ Design ➤ Development ➤ **End Point**

Training need is identified by product management or customer training

Training product approved by product management

tails, allowed the team to get a high-level picture of what the major development steps were. As the team went through the exercise of developing this map, it became clear that the customer training department was developing e-learning without any direct input from the end user of the product.

The next graphical depiction that the team developed was a top-down chart. This map (Figure 12.2) created a simple picture of the e-learning development process identifying two levels of detail. The first level showed the major steps in the process, with the second level showing the subprocesses under each step. This chart gave a little more detail about the existing process even though it did not show delays, decision points, and feedback loops.

FIGURE 12.2. TOP-DOWN CHART OF THE CUSTOMER TRAINING PROCESS.

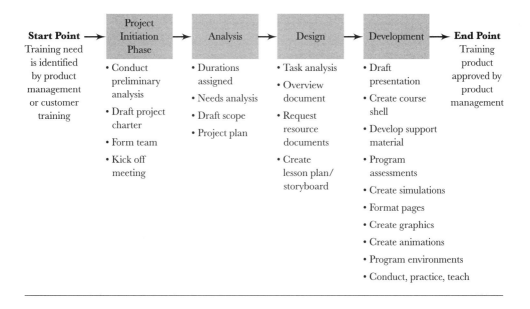

The most difficult and time-consuming graphical depiction of the e-learning process was the functional deployment process map. The team began developing this map with the expectation that it would be a fairly easy process since the team had access to project plans, historical data, and subject matter experts to document what was believed to be occurring in the e-learning development process. As the work to develop the map began, it became quite obvious that what was written on paper and in project plans was not what was actually taking place. This exercise made it clear that not only was there tremendous variation in the e-learning development process, but the people who were involved in e-learning development were not quite sure what tasks should be completed, who was responsible for completing them, and when they should take place.

The functional deployment map took almost four meetings (eight hours) to complete. It required nineteen easel pads two and one half by two feet and covered all the walls of a medium-sized conference room. This detailed map displayed all of the steps in the e-learning development process in sequential order. It illustrated where each step was performed and who was involved. The map clearly displayed that the process contained a series of checks and rechecks that virtually guaranteed rework.

Qualitative Analysis

With the cross-functional process map complete, the team performed a qualitative analysis of the process. The members looked at every step in the e-learning development process and classified each task as customer value added, operational value, not customer value added, or not operational value added. Customer value added was defined as an activity that the customer recognizes as valuable, changes the product toward something that the customer expects, or is done right the first time. Operational value-added activities are activities that are required by contract or other laws and regulations, done right the first time, or required to sustain the workplace ability to perform customer value-added activities.

The team found a significant number of non-value-added activities (NVA) in the e-learning development process. Many of these NVAs were the reviews and approvals required by the various groups within the customer training department and product management. Some were required regardless of whether the reviewer or approving authority was a stakeholder in the deliverable. Removing these activities could potentially reduce the time and cost associated with e-learning development. Many of the steps that are currently accepted as best practices in the training industry were also identified as NVA activities when Six Sigma methodology was applied.

Quick Wins

The NVA activities were then categorized based on whether they were easy to implement, fast to implement, cheap to implement, within the team's control, and easily reversible. The NVA activities that met all of these conditions were identified as quick wins (Table 12.1).

The team then did a failure, mode, effect analysis (FMEA) on each of the activities to determine what failures are occurring and their impact and frequencies. The FMEA validated that removing a step would ultimately do the process more

TABLE 12.1. QUICK WIN EVALUATION MATRIX.

Activity	Easy to Implement: Does Not Require a Great Deal of Coordination	Fast to Implement: Does Not Require a Great Deal of Time	Cheap to Implement: Does Not Require a Great Deal of Time	Within-Team Control	Easily Reversible	Implement: Yes or No
Project initiation phase						
Combine initial meeting with needs analysis	✓		✓	✓	✓	No
Combine charter and SOW	✓	✓	✓	✓	✓	Yes
Eliminate CTIP (IT) review/ approve project charter	✓	✓	✓	✓	✓	No
Eliminate CTIP (training) review/approve project charter	✓	✓	✓	✓	✓	Yes
Eliminate CTIP (documentation) review/approve project charter	✓	✓	✓	✓	✓	Yes
Eliminate PM review/approve project charter	✓	✓	✓	✓	✓	No
Analysis						
Eliminate CTIP review/approve scope	✓	✓	✓	✓	✓	Yes
Eliminate PM review/approve scope	✓	✓	✓	✓	✓	No
Eliminate PM review/approve project plan	✓	✓	✓	✓	✓	No

Note: SOW = scope of work; CTIP = customer training and information products; PM = product manager.

good than harm and also ensured that the proper controls were in place so that removing the step would not cause the process to fail. With the FMEA complete, the team agreed to implement ten quick wins. These quick wins basically removed redundant meetings and multiple levels of reviews and approvals from the process.

Voice of the Customer

With the quick wins identified, the team began to work on defining customer requirements. Six Sigma accomplishes this first by identifying the voice of the customer (VOC). The VOC is then converted to key customer issues, which are in turn converted to critical customer requirements (CCR), or specific measurable targets. The customer training Six Sigma team captured the VOC by reviewing feedback from e-learning course evaluations and sending out surveys asking e-learning customers what was important to them. The team took the customer statements and identified the underlying issues behind them. Those issues were then translated into critical customer requirements. Table 12.2 shows some of the critical customer requirements that were uncovered.

TABLE 12.2. VOC CONVERSION TABLE.

Voice of the Customer: What does the customer want from us?	Key Customer Issues: We need to identify the issue(s) that prevent us from satisfying our customers	Critical Customer Requirements: We should summarize key issues and translate them into specific and measurable requirements
Customer doesn't want to install additional software.	Develop course with software that requires plug-ins.	User experiences are seamless.
The course runs without crashes or hangs.	Pages take more than 20 seconds to load.	Pages take no more than 30 seconds to load.
Screen layout is clear.	Not adhering to design standards.	Adhering to design standards.
Pre- and post-test.	No test.	Courses have quizzes, pre- and post-test.
Be able to enroll using online assistance.	No tutorial.	Enrollment tutorial is available and learner successfully enrolls without additional assistance.
The program (course) should be 2½ to 3 hours.	Poor classroom management techniques.	Ensure practice and teaching meet time and other constraints.

   Using this approach to gather customer requirements was key to the success of the project. This disciplined process prevented individual prejudices from skewing the data. The customer training team found that many of the factors that team members thought were important to end users were not major contributors to customer satisfaction or dissatisfaction. This finding was important since the process map uncovered that much of the e-learning development time was being spent on issues that the team now knew were not important to end users.

Issues Critical to the Process

   The team now knew what customers wanted. The next imperative was to identify business requirements or critical-to-process issues. The broad cross-functional makeup of the Six Sigma team allowed it to quickly identify the customer training e-learning business requirements: that e-learning development time be within 10 percent of the industry standard, rework be less than 10 percent of the overall e-learning development time, and all e-learning deliverables be completed at or below the budgeted cost.

Critical to Quality

   The critical customer requirements and the critical-to-process requirements were then consolidated into a single list that identified all of the measurable criteria that needed to be met in order for the e-learning deliverables to be considered at Six Sigma quality. Six Sigma calls this consolidated list the critical to quality (CTQ). The process is shown in Figure 12.3.

FIGURE 12.3. THE SIX SIGMA MODEL.

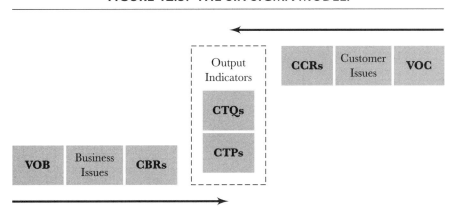

Note: VOB = voice of the business; CBR = critical business requirements; CTP = critical to the process; VOC = voice of the customer; CCR = critical customer requirement; CTQ = critical to quality.

With the critical-to-quality requirements now identified, the team moved into the next phase of the DMAIC model to measure how the customer training department was doing against those requirements.

How Are We Doing? The Measure Phase

To ensure the credibility of the data that would be collected, the team needed to develop a measurement plan (Table 12.3). This plan would dictate what data would be collected, where they would be collected from, how they would be collected, who would collect them, when they would be collected, and most important, operational definitions or clear understandable descriptions of what was to be observed and measured. Once the plan was completed, the measurement began.

Once the data collection was complete, the results were put into Pareto charts, run charts, and histograms, which gave the team a visual representation of the state of e-learning. This representation had both good and bad news. The graphical depiction of how end users felt about the e-learning deliverables was the good news: the data showed that customers were fairly pleased with what they were receiving. This picture was quite different from what was expected by many team members who initially felt that there were quality issues with e-learning deliverables. Figure 12.4 is a Pareto chart of the customer about course navigation, which shows that 100 percent of the respondents either agreed or strongly agreed that the courses were easy to navigate. Figure 12.5 is a Pareto chart showing that 87.5 percent of the customers who responded either agreed or strongly agreed that the exercises contained in the courses were realistic. However, 12.5 percent disagreed.

The data also showed, however, that there was tremendous opportunity for improvement around business requirements or critical-to-process issues. Fifty percent of the e-learning developed took more than 10 percent above industry standard to build. Seventy-four percent of the e-learning developed more than 25 percent of the development time was rework. Figure 12.6 is a process capability analysis, which shows that the mean development time for e-learning courses was 272 hours, but the upper specification limit based on industry standards was only 250 hours.

Figure 12.7 is a process capability analysis for the rework associated with e-learning development. On average, close to 40 percent of development was rework. The current process did not have the capability to meet the target maximum of 25 percent.

The team now had a baseline measure of how the process was performing against both customer and business requirements. It had also identified improvement opportunities. With this information validated, the team then updated the

(text continues on page 201)

TABLE 12.3. MEASUREMENT PLAN.

Performance Measure	Operational Definition	Data Source and Location	Sample Size	Who Will Collect the Data	When Data Will Be Collected	How Data Will Be Collected	Other Data That Should Be Collected at the Same Time
Course is developed within 10 percent of industry standard hours	1 hour e-learning developed in no more than 220 hours 3-hour work-shop developed in no more than 132 hours	Project plans	17 (100 percent) of courses with data	Dana	6/6–6/24	Development hours will be identified from project plan data	Less than 10 percent of development time is associated with rework
Less than 10 percent of development time is associated with rework	No more than 20 rework hours for 1 hour e-earning No more than 12 hours rework for a 3-hour workshop	Project plans	17 (100%) of courses with data	Dana	6/6–6/24	Rework data will be identified from project plan	NA

FIGURE 12.4. CUSTOMER FEEDBACK ON NAVIGATION.

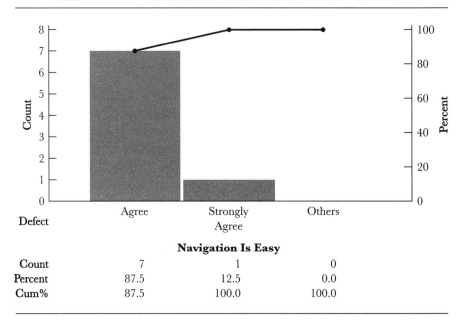

Navigation Is Easy

Defect	Agree	Strongly Agree	Others
Count	7	1	0
Percent	87.5	12.5	0.0
Cum%	87.5	100.0	100.0

FIGURE 12.5. CUSTOMER FEEDBACK ON EXERCISES.

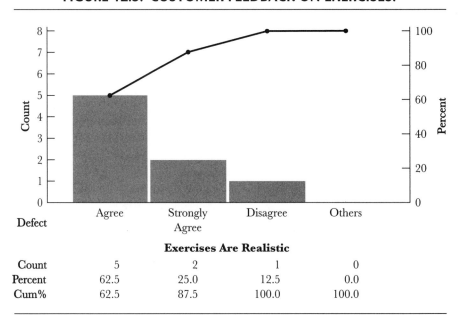

Exercises Are Realistic

Defect	Agree	Strongly Agree	Disagree	Others
Count	5	2	1	0
Percent	62.5	25.0	12.5	0.0
Cum%	62.5	87.5	100.0	100.0

FIGURE 12.6. PROCESS CAPABILITY FOR DEVELOPMENT HOURS.

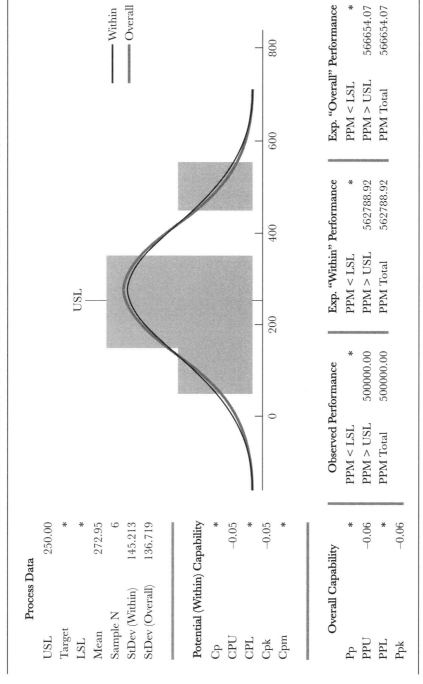

Process Data

USL	250.00
Target	*
LSL	*
Mean	272.95
Sample N	6
StDev (Within)	145.213
StDev (Overall)	136.719

Potential (Within) Capability

Cp	*
CPU	−0.05
CPL	*
Cpk	−0.05
Cpm	*

Overall Capability

Pp	*
PPU	−0.06
PPL	*
Ppk	−0.06

Observed Performance		Exp. "Within" Performance		Exp. "Overall" Performance	
PPM < LSL	*	PPM < LSL	*	PPM < LSL	*
PPM > USL	500000.00	PPM > USL	562788.92	PPM > USL	566654.07
PPM Total	500000.00	PPM Total	562788.92	PPM Total	566654.07

—— Within
—— Overall

FIGURE 12.7. PROCESS CAPABILITY FOR REWORK.

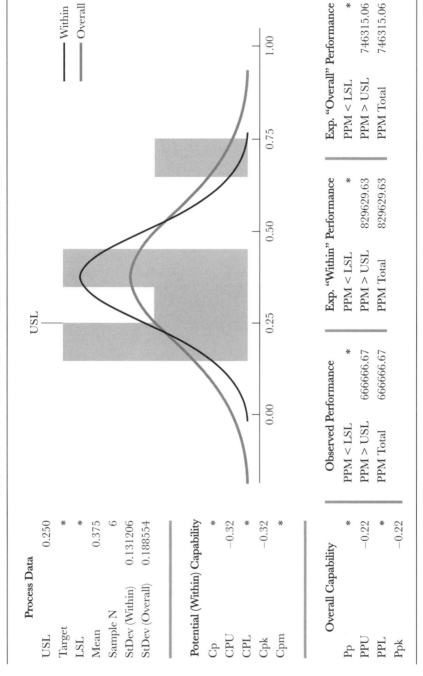

Process Data

USL	0.250
Target	*
LSL	*
Mean	0.375
Sample N	6
StDev (Within)	0.131206
StDev (Overall)	0.188554

Potential (Within) Capability

Cp	*
CPU	−0.32
CPL	*
Cpk	−0.32
Cpm	*

Overall Capability

Pp	*
PPU	−0.22
PPL	*
Ppk	−0.22

Observed Performance		Exp. "Within" Performance		Exp. "Overall" Performance	
PPM < LSL	*	PPM < LSL	*	PPM < LSL	*
PPM > USL	666666.67	PPM > USL	829629.63	PPM > USL	746315.06
PPM Total	666666.67	PPM Total	829629.63	PPM Total	746315.06

USL

—— Within
—— Overall

project goals: "To reduce the annual costs of rework in developing e-learning by 75 percent of the opportunity and to reduce the remaining development time (above the industry standard) by 50 percent of opportunity." The team then moved into the analyze phase, which would allow them to pinpoint and verify exactly what was wrong with the process.

What's Wrong? The Analyze Phase

One of the first tools used during the analysis phase was the process capability analysis. The team wanted to see if the current process even had the capability of meeting the critical to quality (CTQ) requirements. A process capability was done to measure the ability of the process to meet both total development time requirements and percentage rework requirements (Figure 12.8).

The process capability analysis for total development time showed that the current process did not have the ability to meet the critical requirement of being within 10 percent of the industry standard or about 220 hours of development time per hour of e-learning. Even increasing the upper specification limit to 250 hours would have the process failing to meet the requirements 56 percent of the time. Although the mean or average development time was 272 hours, the standard deviation was 136 hours, which verified the amount of variability in the process.

The process capability analysis for rework showed similar results. The current development process did not have the ability to meet the critical requirement of limiting rework to 10 percent of overall development time. Increasing the upper specification limit to 25 percent would have the process failing to meet the requirements 74 percent of the time. Although the mean or average amount of rework was 37 percent, the standard deviation was 18 percent, which again verified the amount of variability in the process.

A more serious discovery that was uncovered during the analyze phase was that while the customer training department was spending upward of 360 hours to design and develop e-learning programs in house, it was spending around 400 hours reviewing and approving e-learning programs that were being developed by vendors. Translated into dollars, it was costing product managers $14,000 just to have the customer training department review and approve courses that were being developed by vendors. Having a vendor develop a one-hour e-learning course was costing product management $71,000 (the cost of the vendor plus the cost of 400 hours spent by customer training personnel to review and approve material).

FIGURE 12.8. PROCESS CAPABILITY FOR ALL DEVELOPMENT HOURS.

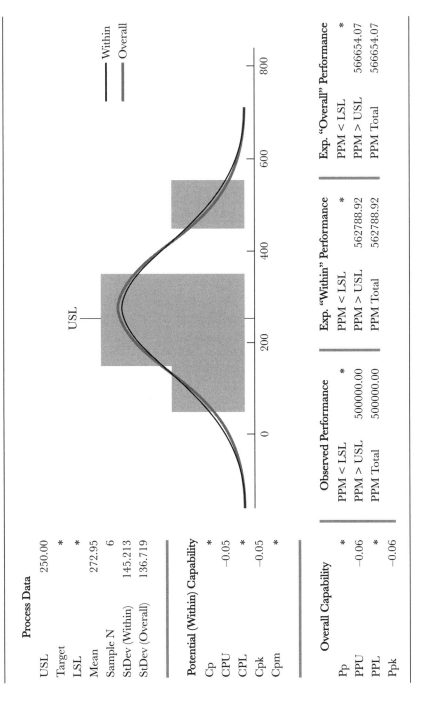

Process Data

USL	250.00
Target	*
LSL	*
Mean	272.95
Sample N	6
StDev (Within)	145.213
StDev (Overall)	136.719

Potential (Within) Capability

Cp	*
CPU	−0.05
CPL	*
Cpk	−0.05
Cpm	*

Overall Capability

Pp	*
PPU	−0.06
PPL	*
Ppk	−0.06

Observed Performance		Exp. "Within" Performance		Exp. "Overall" Performance	
PPM < LSL	*	PPM < LSL	*	PPM < LSL	*
PPM > USL	500000.00	PPM > USL	562788.92	PPM > USL	566654.07
PPM Total	500000.00	PPM Total	562788.92	PPM Total	566654.07

USL

—— Within
—— Overall

With all of this baseline data now available, the team became energized and eager to move into the improve phase and generate solutions for the problems. There was still more analysis to be done, however.

Although Six Sigma relies heavily on statistical data, it has tools that take into account the feelings, hunches, and experiences of team members and subject matter experts. The team next embarked on identifying the root causes of the rework and additional development time. Much of the information about these causes was based on the experiences and recollections of various team members. A series of tools was used to convert the anecdotal data into statistical data and then to validate the data. First, a cause-and-effect or fishbone diagram was developed (Figure 12.9). This diagram allowed the team to explore and graphically display all of the possible causes of rework and development time. It also enabled the team to focus on the content of the problem rather than the history of the problem or the differing personal interests of the team members. In short, it forced the team to focus on causes, not symptoms.

Once all potential root causes of rework and additional development time were identified, the team used multivoting to derive a prioritized list of the root causes and their impact on e-learning development. The results of this prioritization were displayed in a Pareto chart (Figure 12.10).

The team validated its root cause findings by sending out surveys to the designers who worked on the e-learning programs. The results of the survey verified the root cause analysis. Next, a regression analysis was done on the historical data that were available (Figure 12.11). This analysis showed a correlation between the number of resources involved in the design of e-learning and the amount of rework. As the number of people doing e-learning design increased, so did the amount of rework and the percentage of rework. This was quite eye opening since much of the current thinking about e-learning development recommends getting many people involved with the design. The data that the team collected clearly indicated the financial ramifications of that type of model.

The regression analysis also showed that the more resources there were on a project, the more overall hours, the more rework, and the higher the cost. The strongest correlation, however, was the amount of resources in the design phase, with the rework occurring during e-learning development. Putting the data through Pareto charts (Figure 12.12) and Multi-Vari charts (Figure 12.13) verified the results of the regression analysis. (A Multi-Vari chart is an output of doing a multi-variable analysis. This type of analysis provides predictions based on the combined effect of a number of variables.) Thus the analysis showed that additional resources had the greatest impact on project cost and work hours if the additional resources were added in the design phase of the project.

FIGURE 12.9. ROOT CAUSE ANALYSIS REWORK.

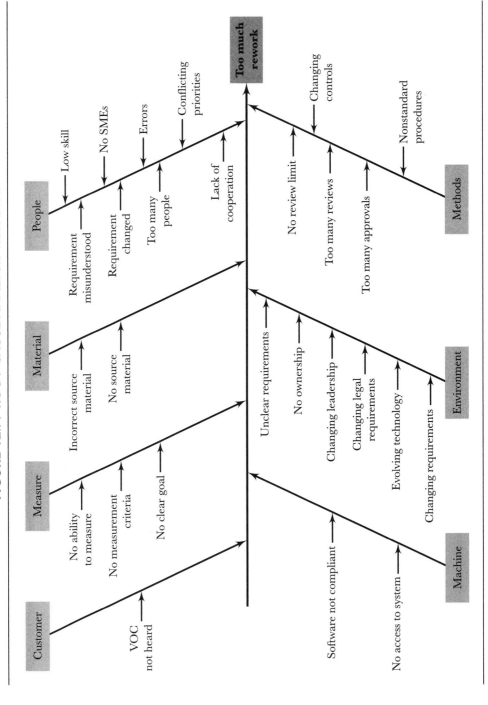

FIGURE 12.10. PARETO CHART OF ROOT CAUSES OF REWORK.

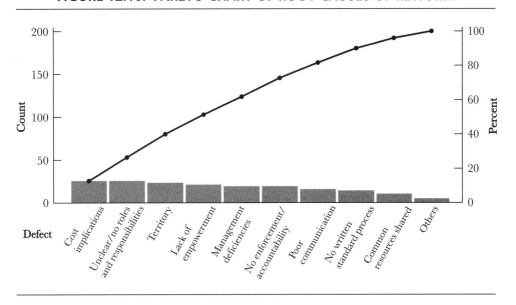

FIGURE 12.11. REGRESSION ANALYSIS OF REWORK.

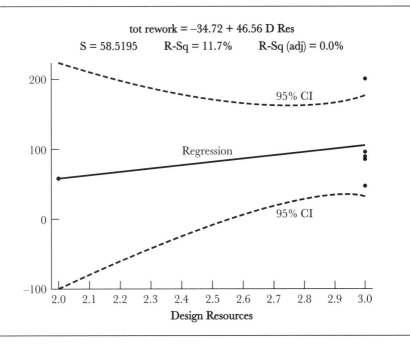

tot rework = −34.72 + 46.56 D Res

S = 58.5195   R-Sq = 11.7%   R-Sq (adj) = 0.0%

FIGURE 12.12. PARETO CHART OF REWORK BY PHASE.

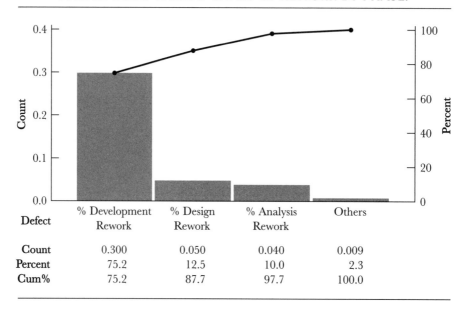

Defect	% Development Rework	% Design Rework	% Analysis Rework	Others
Count	0.300	0.050	0.040	0.009
Percent	75.2	12.5	10.0	2.3
Cum%	75.2	87.7	97.7	100.0

FIGURE 12.13. MULTI-VARI CHART OF HOURS BY RESOURCE.

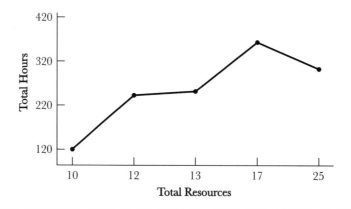

At this point in the process, many team members were concerned about the amount of analysis that was being performed. To a member, however, the team was confident that as a result of the data, any changes made could be validated and justified.

With the root causes identified and verified and the data validated, the team was ready to move into the improve phase, where it would generate solutions for the validated causes of rework and additional development time.

What Do We Need to Do? The Improve Phase

Until this point, the team was focused on gaining greater understanding of the deficiencies affecting the current e-learning development process. This focus gave the team an understanding and validation of the root causes of the deficiencies. The goal of the improve stage is to find and implement solutions that will eliminate those causes. To accomplish this, the team identified, evaluated, selected, and developed solutions using a variety of traditional and nontraditional idea generation tools.

The team generated solutions using a variety of tools, including traditional brainstorming, affinity diagrams, and the random word technique, which allows teams to approach problems from different perspectives as opposed to patterned ways of thinking. The team also employed Edward de Bono's Six Thinking Hats technique. Six Thinking Hats is a powerful brainstorming and decision-making approach. Through this approach, individuals or teams look at decisions from a number of important perspectives and move outside of their habitual thinking style. De Bono's methodology helps teams get a more complete view of a situation.

Once the ideas were generated, the team evaluated the solutions and selected the ones that would have the greatest impact on the goals of the project. To accomplish this, the team developed a cause-and-effect matrix. This tool allowed the team to:

- Remove any solutions that would cause management to stop the project.
- Consider the organizational fit of each solution.
- Narrow the list.
- Develop a solution selection matrix.
- Weight the evaluation criteria.
- Determine the impact the solution would have on the project's goals.
- Evaluate the time benefit of the solution.
- Evaluate the cost impact of the solutions and other impacts.

With the solutions selected, the team conducted FMEA on the solutions. The FMEA validated that controls to make the solutions successful were in place. These controls also became indicators that would allow the team to identify problems and make adjustments long before the rework or additional development time occurred.

Updating the Process

The next step for the team was to use the solutions to update the current process. The original nineteen-page process map was so inundated with decision points, reviews, and approvals that the team agreed to develop a new process map using the solutions that had been generated, as well as what was now known about the process as a guide. The new process map was developed in less than two hours and required only six pages. It highlighted not only each task in the process but who was responsible, who was accountable, who needed to be informed, and who had to review or sign off on the step. It also showed the controls that were in place to ensure that tasks were done right the first time.

The analysis of the solutions projected an 81 percent decrease in rework as well as an 81 percent decrease in the development time that was above the ASTD benchmark. Overall development time was projected to be reduced by 30 percent. These improvements would translate into an annual savings of $282,000.

The Results

The team now had statistical projections indicating the benefit that should be realized based on the Six Sigma solutions. The only way to truly verify that the new process would produce the projected results would be to put it into practice. The new process was applied to three e-learning projects with results shown in Table 12.4: using the process developed with Six Sigma methodology allowed the cus-

TABLE 12.4. RESULTS TABLE.

Project	Course Hours	Development Time (hours)	ASTD Development Time (hours)	Development Time (hours)	ASTD Time (hours)	Percentage Rework
1	1.5	203	300	135	200	8
2	2.0	220	400	110	200	8
3	2.5	350	500	140	200	12

tomer training department to develop e-learning programs in significantly less time than the industry average.

A comparison of critical-to-process issues before and after the Six Sigma improvements were implemented shows the dramatic improvements even more clearly (Figure 12.14).

FIGURE 12.14. IMPROVEMENTS AS A RESULT OF SIX SIGMA.

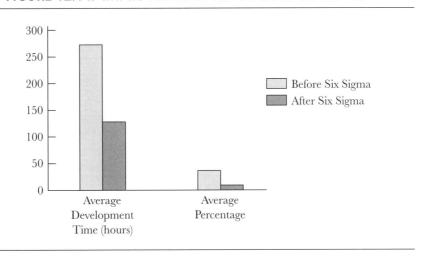

Finally, a process capability analysis on the new process shows that it now has the ability to meet and the development time requirements 84 percent of the time. Moreover, the standard deviation is now 18 as opposed to the 145 hours prior to applying Six Sigma methodology.

How Do We Guarantee Performance? The Control Phase

The team had validated the improvements and documented that they worked. The team also verified that the new development process was stable and capable of meeting the critical-to-quality requirements. The last phase of Six Sigma is the control phase, where the performance of the process is routinely measured to ensure that critical customer requirements continue to be met.

The root cause analysis that was performed during the project identified for the team which key outputs needed to be measured. The failure mode and effects

FIGURE 12.15. PROCESS CAPABILITY AFTER SIX SIGMA.

Process Data

USL	220.000
Target	*
LSL	*
Mean	128.333
Sample N	3
StDev (Within)	24.3794
StDev (Overall)	18.1362

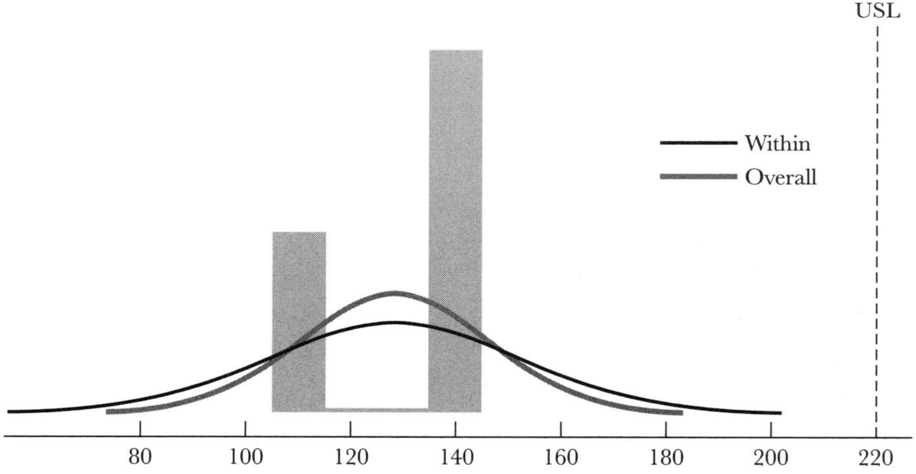

Potential (Within) Capability

Cp	*
CPU	1.25
CPL	*
Cpk	1.25
Cpm	*

Overall Capability

Pp	*
PPU	1.68
PPL	*
Ppk	1.68

Observed Performance		Exp. "Within" Performance		Exp. "Overall" Performance	
PPM < LSL	*	PPM < LSL	*	PPM < LSL	*
PPM > USL	0.00	PPM > USL	84.96	PPM > USL	0.22
PPM Total	0.00	PPM Total	84.96	PPM Total	0.22

analysis uncovered the action to be taken in the event that a measured output was outside its control limit. A tracking log was set up to measure these outputs, and the results of this log are reported to executive management every six months.

A Final Thought

Doing e-learning the Six Sigma way has allowed DTCC's customer training department to identify and exceed critical customer and business requirements for e-learning, reduce overall development time by close to 50 percent, reduce annual development costs by $282,000, and articulate e-learning in a way that business managers understand. Perhaps just as important as the savings and the identification of customer and business requirements is the ability that the customer training department now has to maintain this high level of performance.

REFERENCES

Accenture. (2004). *The rise of the high-performance learning organization.* Available at http://www. accenture.com/global/services/by_subject/workforce_performance/r_and_i/the organi zation.htm

Bloom B. S. (1956). *Taxonomy of educational objectives, Handbook I: The cognitive domain.* New York: McKay.

Breakthrough Management Group Transactional DFSS Course. Available at http://www.bmgi.com/methodologies/methodologies_dfss.aspx

Clark, D. *Introduction to instructional systems design.* Available at http://www.nwlink. com/~donclark/hrd/sat1.html/

Gagné, R. (1965). *The conditions of learning and the theory of instruction.* Belmont, CA: Wadsworth.

ICF Consulting. Available at http://www.icfconsulting.com/Services/Training/trng-isd.asp/

Kirkpatrick, D. L. (1959a). Techniques for evaluating training programs. *Journal of the American Society of Training Directors, 13*(11), 3-9.

Kirkpatrick, D. L. (1959b). Techniques for evaluating training programs: Part Two—Learning. *Journal of the American Society of Training Directors, 13*(12), 21-26.

Kirkpatrick, D. L. (1960a). Techniques for evaluating training programs: Part Three— Behavior. *Journal of the American Society of Training Directors, 14*(1), 13-18.

Kirkpatrick, D. L. (1960b). Techniques for evaluating training programs: Part Four—Results. *Journal of the American Society of Training Directors, 14*(2), 28-32.

Kirkpatrick, D. L. (1975). Techniques for evaluating programs (Parts 1, 2, 3, and 4). *Evaluating Training Programs: A Collection of Articles from the Journal of the American Society for Training and Development.* Madison, Wis.: ASTD.

Kruse, K. *Gagné's nine events of instruction: An introduction.* Available at http://www.e-learning guru.com/articles/art3_3.htm

San Jose State Instructional Design Program. Available at www.imperial.edu/de/downloads_inst/instructional_design/ADDIE.pdf

Skinner, B. F. (1954). The science of learning and the art of teaching. *Harvard Educational Review, 24,* 86-97.

Southern Illinois University. Available at http://www.siue.edu/~dknowlt/IT510/IT510_main.html/

van Adelsberg, D. & Trolley, E. A. (1999). *Running training like a business: Delivering unmistakable value.* San Francisco: Berrett-Koehler.

INDEX

ABOUT THE AUTHOR

Kaliym A. Islam is the director of learning product development and technology services for the Depository Trust & Clearing Corporation. He received his Six Sigma Black Belt from Motorola and is an advocate for positioning learning organizations as business units in order to enhance their credibility and value to organizations. Kaliym is vice-president of MetroSet, a consortium dedicated to technology education and a member of the advisory board of the Chief Learning Officer Institute

Kaliym is a featured contributing writer to LTI NewsLine and has published a number of articles. He has been a keynote presenter on the subject of the application of business approaches to training development at a number of industry conferences. A former educator in the New York City public schools, Kaliym has been the recipient of the Gift of Time Award, as well as the Horace E. Green Award. He has been cited by the City Council of New York for his innovative work as an educator and by the Jackie Robinson Center for Physical Culture for his educational leadership. Recently he was named to the Manchester Who's Who of Executives.

Pfeiffer Publications Guide

This guide is designed to familiarize you with the various types of Pfeiffer publications. The formats section describes the various types of products that we publish; the methodologies section describes the many different ways that content might be provided within a product. We also provide a list of the topic areas in which we publish.

FORMATS

In addition to its extensive book-publishing program, Pfeiffer offers content in an array of formats, from fieldbooks for the practitioner to complete, ready-to-use training packages that support group learning.

FIELDBOOK Designed to provide information and guidance to practitioners in the midst of action. Most fieldbooks are companions to another, sometimes earlier, work, from which its ideas are derived; the fieldbook makes practical what was theoretical in the original text. Fieldbooks can certainly be read from cover to cover. More likely, though, you'll find yourself bouncing around following a particular theme, or dipping in as the mood, and the situation, dictate.

HANDBOOK A contributed volume of work on a single topic, comprising an eclectic mix of ideas, case studies, and best practices sourced by practitioners and experts in the field.

An editor or team of editors usually is appointed to seek out contributors and to evaluate content for relevance to the topic. Think of a handbook not as a ready-to-eat meal, but as a cookbook of ingredients that enables you to create the most fitting experience for the occasion.

RESOURCE Materials designed to support group learning. They come in many forms: a complete, ready-to-use exercise (such as a game); a comprehensive resource on one topic (such as conflict management) containing a variety of methods and approaches; or a collection of like-minded activities (such as icebreakers) on multiple subjects and situations.

TRAINING PACKAGE An entire, ready-to-use learning program that focuses on a particular topic or skill. All packages comprise a guide for the facilitator/trainer and a workbook for the participants. Some packages are supported with additional media—such as video—or learning aids, instruments, or other devices to help participants understand concepts or practice and develop skills.

- *Facilitator/trainer's guide* Contains an introduction to the program, advice on how to organize and facilitate the learning event, and step-by-step instructor notes. The guide also contains copies of presentation materials—handouts, presentations, and overhead designs, for example—used in the program.

- *Participant's workbook* Contains exercises and reading materials that support the learning goal and serves as a valuable reference and support guide for participants in the weeks and months that follow the learning event. Typically, each participant will require his or her own workbook.

ELECTRONIC CD-ROMs and Web-based products transform static Pfeiffer content into dynamic, interactive experiences. Designed to take advantage of the searchability, automation, and ease-of-use that technology provides, our e-products bring convenience and immediate accessibility to your workspace.

METHODOLOGIES

CASE STUDY A presentation, in narrative form, of an actual event that has occurred inside an organization. Case studies are not prescriptive, nor are they used to prove a point; they are designed to develop critical analysis and decision-making skills. A case study has a specific time frame, specifies a sequence of events, is narrative in structure, and contains a plot structure—an issue (what should be/have been done?). Use case studies when the goal is to enable participants to apply previously learned theories to the circumstances in the case, decide what is pertinent, identify the real issues, decide what should have been done, and develop a plan of action.

ENERGIZER A short activity that develops readiness for the next session or learning event. Energizers are most commonly used after a break or lunch to stimulate or refocus the group. Many involve some form of physical activity, so they are a useful way to counter post-lunch lethargy. Other uses include transitioning from one topic to another, where "mental" distancing is important.

EXPERIENTIAL LEARNING ACTIVITY (ELA) A facilitator-led intervention that moves participants through the learning cycle from experience to application (also known as a Structured Experience). ELAs are carefully thought-out designs in which there is a definite learning purpose and intended outcome. Each step—everything that participants do during the activity—facilitates the accomplishment of the stated goal. Each ELA includes complete instructions for facilitating the intervention and a clear statement of goals, suggested group size and timing, materials required, an explanation of the process, and, where appropriate, possible variations to the activity. (For more detail on Experiential Learning Activities, see the Introduction to the *Reference Guide to Handbooks and Annuals*, 1999 edition, Pfeiffer, San Francisco.)

GAME A group activity that has the purpose of fostering team spirit and togetherness in addition to the achievement of a pre-stated goal. Usually contrived—undertaking a desert expedition, for example—this type of learning method offers an engaging means for participants to demonstrate and practice business and interpersonal skills. Games are effective for team building and personal development mainly because the goal is subordinate to the process—the means through which participants reach decisions, collaborate, communicate, and generate trust and understanding. Games often engage teams in "friendly" competition.

ICEBREAKER A (usually) short activity designed to help participants overcome initial anxiety in a training session and/or to acquaint the participants with one another. An icebreaker can be a fun activity or can be tied to specific topics or training goals. While a useful tool in itself, the icebreaker comes into its own in situations where tension or resistance exists within a group.

INSTRUMENT A device used to assess, appraise, evaluate, describe, classify, and summarize various aspects of human behavior. The term used to describe an instrument depends primarily on its format and purpose. These terms include survey, questionnaire, inventory, diagnostic, survey, and poll. Some uses of instruments include providing instrumental feedback to group members, studying here-and-now processes or functioning within a group, manipulating group composition, and evaluating outcomes of training and other interventions.

Instruments are popular in the training and HR field because, in general, more growth can occur if an individual is provided with a method for focusing specifically on his or her own behavior. Instruments also are used to obtain information that will serve as a basis for change and to assist in workforce planning efforts.

Paper-and-pencil tests still dominate the instrument landscape with a typical package comprising a facilitator's guide, which offers advice on administering the instrument and interpreting the collected data, and an initial set of instruments. Additional instruments are available separately. Pfeiffer, though, is investing heavily in e-instruments. Electronic instrumentation provides effortless distribution and, for larger groups particularly, offers advantages over paper-and-pencil tests in the time it takes to analyze data and provide feedback.

LECTURETTE A short talk that provides an explanation of a principle, model, or process that is pertinent to the participants' current learning needs. A lecturette is intended to establish a common language bond between the trainer and the participants by providing a mutual frame of reference. Use a lecturette as an introduction to a group activity or event, as an interjection during an event, or as a handout.

MODEL A graphic depiction of a system or process and the relationship among its elements. Models provide a frame of reference and something more tangible, and more easily remembered, than a verbal explanation. They also give participants something to "go on," enabling them to track their own progress as they experience the dynamics, processes, and relationships being depicted in the model.

ROLE PLAY A technique in which people assume a role in a situation/scenario: a customer service rep in an angry-customer exchange, for example. The way in which the role is approached is then discussed and feedback is offered. The role play is often repeated using a different approach and/or incorporating changes made based on feedback received. In other words, role playing is a spontaneous interaction involving realistic behavior under artificial (and safe) conditions.

SIMULATION A methodology for understanding the interrelationships among components of a system or process. Simulations differ from games in that they test or use a model that depicts or mirrors some aspect of reality in form, if not necessarily in content. Learning occurs by studying the effects of change on one or more factors of the model. Simulations are commonly used to test hypotheses about what happens in a system—often referred to as "what if?" analysis—or to examine best-case/worst-case scenarios.

THEORY A presentation of an idea from a conjectural perspective. Theories are useful because they encourage us to examine behavior and phenomena through a different lens.

TOPICS

The twin goals of providing effective and practical solutions for workforce training and organization development and meeting the educational needs of training and human resource professionals shape Pfeiffer's publishing program. Core topics include the following:

Leadership & Management

Communication & Presentation

Coaching & Mentoring

Training & Development

e-Learning

Teams & Collaboration

OD & Strategic Planning

Human Resources

Consulting

What will you find on pfeiffer.com?

- The best in workplace performance solutions for training and HR professionals

- Downloadable training tools, exercises, and content

- Web-exclusive offers

- Training tips, articles, and news

- Seamless online ordering

- Author guidelines, information on becoming a Pfeiffer Affiliate, and much more

Discover more at www.pfeiffer.com